NEW YORK REVIEW BOOKS
CLASSICS

THE JEFFERSONIAN
TRANSFORMATION

HENRY ADAMS (1838–1918), a lineal descendant of presidents John Adams and John Quincy Adams, grew up in Massachusetts, graduated from Harvard College, and served during the Civil War as secretary to his father, Charles Francis Adams, who was the US ambassador to Great Britain at the time. Returning to Washington from England 1868, Adams was deeply dismayed by the politics of the Reconstruction Era and renounced any political ambitions of his own, dedicating himself instead to a career of writing and teaching. From 1870 to 1877, Adams lectured on history at Harvard while editing *The North American Review*. He then moved back to Washington, his primary residence for the rest of his life. In 1880 Adams published *Democracy*, an anonymous novel about American politics, and in 1884 *Esther*, a New York story which appeared under the pseudonym of Frances Snow Compton. Biographies of Albert Gallatin (1879) and John Randolph (1889) reflected a profound knowledge of the early history of the American Republic that culminated in the nine volumes of the *History of the United States of America Under the Administrations of Jefferson and Madison*, which came out between 1889 and 1891. Adams's marriage to Marian Hooper in 1872 ended with her suicide in 1888, an event which left him distraught. In later years Adams advocated a deterministic theory of history, which he sought to establish as a hard science on the model of physics. This view finds remarkable expression in the two eccentric masterpieces of Adams's old age, Mont Saint-Michel and Chartres and the autobiographical Education of Henry Adams, privately printed in 1907 and only released to the public following Adams's death in 1918.

GARRY WILLS is Professor of History Emeritus at Northwestern. His most recent book, *What Jesus Meant*, was published in 2006.

THE JEFFERSONIAN TRANSFORMATION

Passages from the "History"

HENRY ADAMS

Introduction by
GARRY WILLS

NEW YORK REVIEW BOOKS

New York

THIS IS A NEW YORK REVIEW BOOK
PUBLISHED BY THE NEW YORK REVIEW OF BOOKS
1755 Broadway, New York, NY 10019
www.nyrb.com

Library of Congress Cataloging-in-Publication Data
Adams, Henry, 1838–1918.
 [History of the United States of America. Selections]
 The Jeffersonian transformation / by Henry Adams ; introduction by
Garry Wills.
    p. cm.
 ISBN-13: 978-1-59017-215-5 (alk. paper)
 ISBN-10: 1-59017-215-9 (alk. paper)
 1. United States—History—1801–1809. 2. United States—History—1809–1817.
3. United States—Politics and government—1801–1809. 4. United States—
Politics and government—1809–1817. 5. Jefferson, Thomas, 1743–1826.
6. Madison, James, 1751–1836. I. Title.
 E302.1.A2535 2006
 973.4'6—dc22

                            2006015634

ISBN-13: 978-1-59017-215-5
ISBN-10: 1-59017-215-9

Printed in the United States of America on acid-free paper.
10 9 8 7 6 5 4 3 2 1

CONTENTS

INTRODUCTION

The Mystery of the Missing Masterpiece

Between the two poles of Henry Adams's life—between an "Adamsy" beginning, in his famous family, and the posthumous *Education of Henry Adams*, on which his later fame is based—there is a mysterious blank. It might be called "The Mystery of the Missing Masterpiece." The great work of his middle years, to which he devoted decades of intense creativity, is an achievement neglected or misrepresented. Some think, mistakenly, that he aspired to a presidential career, like that of his great-grandfather and grandfather, John Adams and John Quincy Adams—but he did not. He recoiled from public life. He gave only one public lecture as an adult, and regretted that. He conceived what, in his eyes, was a far greater ambition. In Europe after his graduation from Harvard, he sat on the steps in Rome where Edward Gibbon said he conceived the idea of his *Decline and Fall of the Roman Empire*, and felt the call to achieve something on that scale for American history.

The wonder is that he fulfilled this high ambition. He prepared himself for it in careful stages. He circled his subject with research carried on in four (eventually five) countries. He chose his period carefully, and wrote five volumes of ancillary work on the period. Then he wrote nine volumes of narrative history covering sixteen years at the beginning of the nineteenth century—*The History of the United States During the Administrations of Thomas Jefferson* (four volumes) and *The History of the United States During the Administrations of James*

Madison (five volumes). Published between 1889 and 1891, these books are brilliant in method and in style. They are the non-fiction prose masterpiece of nineteenth-century America. That is the wonder—almost the miracle.

The mystery is that his great accomplishment fell into obscurity—it was out of print through most of the twentieth century. There was a quiet but powerful resistance to both the subject and the author. Gibbon had described the decline and fall of the Roman Empire. Adams traced the rise and triumph of an American empire. It was not a story that people wanted to hear. Some denied that there was any such thing as the rise and triumph of an American empire. Others felt that, if there was such a thing, it did not occur when Adams said it did. Still others said that if it did occur then, he was the wrong person to prove that it did.

The resistance to the *History* came in the form of a pincer movement, operating from two directions—one from before the *History*, connected with his family, the other coming from after the *History*, connected with his late masterpiece, *The Education of Henry Adams*. The first group thinks that Henry Adams is first and always an Adams, always speaking for his family. The second group thinks that Adams is always and only the Adams of the *Education*, disillusioned and satirical. These two attitudes converged, for different reasons, on the same part of the *History*, the first six chapters of the first volume on Jefferson's terms (which Adams called his "administrations"). These chapters provide a thick description of a single year, 1800, and they are often hailed as a pioneer work of social history. They have even been printed separately. They are the most-read part of the larger work—often the only part read, since reading them is now simply a substitute for reading the whole *History*. Reading them is a kind of antidote to the rest, an apotropaic entry-point to warn people from going farther. The way people treat them reminds me of an artifact I saw in the Museum of Modern Art in the 1970s, a box with a big button that said PUSH ME. When you pushed it, the box sprang open, a hand came up from inside and pulled the lid shut again. The opening chapters of the *History* were made to function like that.

Those six chapters describe an America compartmentalized and backward-looking, resistant to ideas, to inventions, to experiment, and to technology. For their own reasons, those coming at the work from Adams's earlier life seize on this section and say, "See! That is what the whole *History* is going to be like, an attack on the Jeffersonians who had opposed his forebears." Those looking back from the *Education* say, "See! He was already the Adams of the *Education*, satirical about his own country." The great historian Richard Hofstadter said that Adams deliberately chose a low mean period of American history so he could castigate it. He describes the whole work in words that apply only to its opening—"an age of slack and derivative culture, of fumbling and small-minded statecraft, terrible parochial wrangling and treasonous schemes." Why would he want to devote the prime of his life to trashing such a worthless object? Hafstadter said it was an act of family revenge.

Noble Cunningham, a respected biographer of Jefferson, delivered a series of lectures published as a book—*The United States in 1800: Henry Adams Revisited*—which treats the six chapters as an unfair denigration of Jefferson. But it is clear from Cunningham's text that he never bothered to read the last four chapters of the final volume. Those chapters celebrate the different America that was produced by the intervening sixteen years. It is an America that has new unity and purpose, an America that is forward-looking, intellectually vibrant, and religiously tolerant, one that has slipped free of the old straitjackets of ideology (whether Federalist or Republican).

Many other historians and literary critics have made the same mistake as Hofstadter and Cunningham. It is a scandal that this should be so. They take the initial chapters as a preview of all the volumes that follow them, overlooking the most obvious point, that opening's announced subject, the state of America in the year 1800—the year *before Jefferson took office.* Adams is describing the condition left behind by the Federalists, the America that John Adams was still presiding over. Henry Adams gives this as a starting point from which the Republicans are going to propel the nation. Adams is not defending his forebears. He is saying that they made a mess of things. He had already written, in his life of John Randolph, that President Adams's unconstitutional Alien and Sedition Acts proved that "it was time that opposition should be put in power." He proposed to teach American history at Harvard by letting his prize graduate student, Henry Cabot Lodge, expound the Federalist position, since he (Henry) had no sympathy for it. He told the students that "John Adams was a demagogue," and called John Quincy Adams "demonic" in his family relations and opportunist in his politics. Adams's brother Charles objected to the harsh criticism of John Quincy in the *History* itself, and Henry prevented his brother Brooks from publishing a biography that praised John Quincy.

Adams and Jefferson

There is no truth to the common assumption that Adams was hostile to Jefferson. In his life of Gallatin, Adams wrote about the only two presidents he called great: "Washington and Jefferson doubtless stand pre-eminent as the representatives of what is best in our national character or its aspirations." Adams felt an affinity with Jefferson, in terms of temperament and policy. They were both aesthetes and art collectors. They both exercised great care in creating their beautiful homes. They were Anglophobes and Francophiles. They preferred the warm-hearted South to the frigid North. Adams no less than Jefferson abhorred a national debt and distrusted banks. Both men fancied themselves as amateur scientists, though each took an aesthetic approach to science that real scientists (David Rittenhouse in Jefferson's case and Charles Lyell in Adams's) disdained.

Adams will criticize some of Jefferson's actions, especially those undertaken to enforce the national Embargo. But he is never as severe on Jefferson as on the Adams presidents. He never doubted Jefferson's sincerity or idealism, and he thought the idealism was ultimately beneficial to the nation. When Jefferson creates a stronger national government, against his own stated hope of reducing central authority, Adams does not ascribe this to an appetite for power. Jefferson found that his own ideals of an American destiny, of a national (not a sectional) party, of the participation of the American people in politics, were ends that could not be reached by the means he preferred, and—as usually happens—the ends prevailed over the expected means. Adams was happy that they did.

Step by step Jefferson was led to bringing about a greater sense of common effort in all of the people. Though he was opposed on principle to using government patronage, he could not create a national party unless he rewarded the new Republicans in states like Pennsylvania and New York. His support of the Twelfth Amendment, making the vice president subordinate to the president on a unified ticket, led to region-balancing, another nationalizing move. Jefferson had to buy Louisiana, despite his constitutional misgivings (he might have been impeached if he turned down such a bargain), and then he had to govern the new territory with unprecedented executive powers. Even his Embargo, meant to keep the nation out of war, prepared it for war by Jefferson's mobilization of the army to enforce it. Adams sees the result of Republican rule as a benign comedy of errors. "T. J. is a case for Beaumarchais, he needs the lightest of touches."

The Education of Henry Adams tells the story of a man

continually trying to get an education and failing. He failed, he says, as a teacher, as a journalist, as an editor, as a historian. None of that was true. When the book was posthumously published, his students, now leaders in their fields, protested vehemently, saying he was the most inspiring teacher they had encountered. He won acclaim in all the fields where he presents himself as a ludicrous object (partly to take the sting out of the mockery he directs at other people). The *History* has a different form of irony. Jefferson keeps trying to fail at making a nation, but keeps on succeeding.

In the *History*, Adams celebrates nationalism and democracy, he is optimistic about America as a world power, he rejoices in the progress that was made in communication, transportation, and scientific experiment. Much of this he attributes to the discipline developed for fighting the War of 1812, which led to organization of resources, professionalizing of the military, perfection of fortifications, and glorious naval exploits. He is especially proud of the navy, despite the fact that he was not a sailor himself and was sick every time he crossed either ocean. He loves the ships and their makers, the improbable defeats inflicted on the proud British navy. He admires the military heroes who gave the nation a common pride—five later presidents of the United States had fought in the War of 1812, as did many who won lower offices.

The New History

It is an exciting story Adams tells, spread out on a grand scale. It is a monument of the new history introduced in the nineteenth century, scientific history as opposed to the philosophical history that was written in the eighteenth century. Adams saw the opening of archives in Europe as a great opportunity. By dint of his fortune and connections, he was the first to get at these troves—in London, in Paris, in Madrid, in Seville. In that pre-Xerox age, he had an army of scribes following in his track, copying the passages he noted for transcription. He bought great quantities of paper, of uniform size, so he could bind all the documents in chronological order, archive by archive. The result was twenty large volumes of original material now resting in the Library of Congress.

Adams discovered many things from these journeys. He learned, for instance, what Napoleon meant to do with Louisiana before his Caribbean ambitions were checked by the black revolutionary in Haiti, Toussaint Louverture. Adams was especially excited by his findings on the Aaron Burr conspiracy. Burr was charged with trying to separate western regions from the Union. He denied that, saying he just raised troops to fight if war came with Mexico. Hard proof was absent until Adams found it. He uncovered the dispatches sent by European diplomats to their home government, telling how Burr approached them with the plan to break the West away if their governments would give him the money to accomplish it. (Some of the emissaries recommended that the governments pay up.) This was such a hot discovery that Adams could not wait to work it into the *History*. Like any researcher with a breathtaking discovery, he wanted to get the story out right away, so he wrote a brief biography of Aaron Burr, using the new material. He offered the book to the Great American Statesman series in which he had already published his biography of John Randolph. The publisher turned it down, saying Aaron Burr was not a great American statesman but a scoundrel. (Adams thought one could be both.) He considered sending the book to a New York publisher, but by the time he could do that he was already working his fresh information into the *History*, so he decided to suppress the biography.

Reading the "History"

The length of the *History* is daunting, but it is fascinating wherever one picks it up. Sections can be read as little masterpieces in their own right—the story of the Burr conspiracy, or the history of the War of 1812, or the many passages where Jefferson and Napoleon (the two giants of the age in Adams's eyes) fence with each other for the Floridas. The stages of the history are well marked. Adams planned the series to have a simple symmetry. He would devote two volumes to each of Jefferson's terms, making four volumes for the entire eight years of his presidency. Then he would repeat the same scheme for Madison's eight years. But the complexity of operations in the War of 1812 could not be crammed into the fourth volume devoted to Madison, so a fifth book had to be added. The whole is rounded off, at either end, by a survey of the state of the nation before and after the Republicans solidified their hold on the government. I have already pointed out how dangerous it was to treat the opening chapters as a separate unit, how that became a preventative for reading the whole. Some of that curse can be taken off by printing those chapters paired with the book-end chapters from the conclusion of volume nine. I hope that consideration of them together may be a spur to reading how Adams traced the path from one state to the other, rather than as a way of skipping the heart of the tale. Here, then, I will look at the merits of each section in itself and in combination with its partner.

The Opening Chapters

The idea of doing a deep social survey of the nation came to Adams in 1876, the last of his six years as editor of the *North American Review*. To mark the centennial of the Declaration of

Independence, he asked six experts to gauge the condition of the republic at the end of its first century. He asked for candor and depth. He did not want patriotic boosting, but scholarly assessment. He chose writers he thought best qualified to make that kind of survey in their separate fields. The areas to be covered were: Religion, Politics, Abstract Science, Economic Science, Law, and Education. He meant to run an article on a seventh subject, Literature, but his first choice as author of it, his colleague at Harvard, James Russell Lowell, turned him down, and his second choice, Thomas Lounsbery of Yale, did not finish the article in time. The national report card submitted was generally hopeful without being superficially optimistic (as were most celebrations of the centennial). Adams's own centennial contribution to the magazine was more celebratory—the refutation of a German historian's conclusion that the American Constitution was a failure.

By creating the 1876 survey, Adams had already established and reflected on the kinds of categories he could use in surveying the state of the nation at the end of the Federalist era. He first lays down a statistical basis for evaluation—the geographic, demographic, and economic situation of each of the three main regions he considers (Northern, Middle, and Southern states). In his reform journalism, he had turned to the census and tax reports in Washington for analyses of the economic health of the nation. That was an experience he put to good use in the *History*. He had another model for his survey, the famous third chapter of Thomas Babington Macaulay's *History of England*, which described "The State of New England in 1685." Macaulay, too, began his work with statistics, but built on them a superstructure assessing the religious, intellectual, and artistic state of the nation, region by region. Adams was able to do the same thing, using a wider variety of sources than were available to Macaulay.

Adams breaks down each of his three main regions into

subdivisions. In the North he finds two different cultures centered in Massachusetts and Connecticut. A similar division in the Middle Region exists between New York and Pennsylvania. In the South, he distinguishes Virginia from the Deep South. The North, his own area, is described as deeply conservative in religion, education, and the arts. The use of religion for political purposes (to fend off Republicanism) was emptying it of its authenticity:

> Nothing tended so directly to make respectability conservative and conservatism a fetich of respectability as this union of bench and pulpit. The democrat had no caste; he was not respectable; he was a Jacobin,—and no such character was admitted into a Federalist house.

Virginia is the most advanced state in its political ideals and practice, as typified by its admirable leaders—George Washington, John Marshall, George Wythe, George Mason, Thomas Jefferson, and James Madison. But it was as backward as its more southern neighbors in all things connected with the slave economy. Its one university was somnolent, its church corrupt:

> Debarred from manufactures, possessed of no shipping, and enjoying no domestic market, Virginian energies necessarily knew no other resource than agriculture. Without church, university, schools, or literature in any form that required or fostered intellectual life, the Virginians concentrated their thought almost exclusively upon politics; and in this concentration produced a result so distinct and lasting, and in character so respectable, that American history would lose no small part of its interest in losing the Virginia school.

This hypertrophy of political skills, when joined with the

pragmatism of Pennsylvania and the opening to the West, held a promise of what the Jeffersonians would achieve in the coming years—though Adams delays making this prediction until he can describe it as confirmed at the end of volume nine.

In the Middle Region, New York has a rather deracinated commercialism, after the fading of its Dutch heritage, but New Jersey has the Scottish Enlightenment burgeoning at Princeton under John Witherspoon. Pennsylvania, however, is the region that merits most of Adams's praise. It has a pragmatic understanding of democracy, relatively free from the rigid ideologies of the North and the South. Philadelphia is the city in America most attuned to Enlightenment secularism, harbinger of what Adams will be praising throughout America by 1817. The city is gentled under Quaker influence, so often praised by Enlightenment heroes like Voltaire: "With twenty different religious creeds, its practice could not be narrow, and a strong Quaker element made it humane." It was "easy, tolerant, and contented," with a rational urban policy and an interest in science symbolized by the great astronomer David Rittenhouse. It was the center of medical education and practice in the United States, with hospitals, penal experiments, homes for the insane, and leading physicians like John Morgan, William Shippen, Caspar Wistar, Philip Syng Physick, and Benjamin Rush. It was the first center of abolitionist activity. Even in literature it emitted the first genuinely American voices. While New England indulged in pale simulacra of the Augustan poets of England, Hugh Henry Brackenridge was writing a racy vernacular version of *Don Quixote*, a signal of the energies that would be generated on the western frontier. The first American novelist of any importance was Charles Brockden Brown, of a Quaker Philadelphia family.

If you asked anyone before he or she read the opening chapters of the *History* what part of the nation he would consider the most promising, few would name the Pennsylvania region.

Popular histories favor either the Northern intellectual bastions of the Federalists or the Southern plantations of the Republicans. But it is important to Adams's view of America that he considered both of those as retrograde extremes, opposed to the area that struck a medium between them. He was, of course, intimate with the Pennsylvania experience from his immersion in the Albert Gallatin papers. But Pennsylvania also offered him a field for one of his favorite intellectual exercises, that of paradox.

Philadelphia was the most cosmopolitan city in America, which meant that it was in close contact with Europe—with the medical schools in Scotland, with the Philadelphia painters flocking to Benjamin West's studio in London, with the French contacts Franklin cultivated. Yet the most sophisticated and worldly society on this continent was also the most deeply American section, that most oriented to the West and to the New World's own experience. By the end of the period his *History* covers, Adams will see an America no longer (with the Federalists) treating England as a model and France as a bugbear, no longer (with the Republicans) treating France as a model and England as a bugbear. Already Pennsylvania had reached the stage of seeing Europe as a partner, not an antagonist. The Jeffersonians will usher the nation into a new world during the course of the *History*, but that new world will look surprisingly like Pennsylvania.

The social history of the opening chapters is also a proleptic vision of the *History*'s last chapters. In the sixth and last of his opening chapters, Adams wrote a passage that Noble Cunningham considered out of place and inexplicable in his dreary "attack" on Jeffersonian America. Conservative and sluggish as America was in 1800, it did not have the deeper burdens of conservatism weighing Europe down:

American society might be both sober and sad, but except for Negro slavery it was sound and healthy in every part. Stripped for the hardest work, every muscle firm and elastic, every ounce of brain ready for use, and not a trace of superfluous flesh on his nervous and supple body, the American stood in the world a new order of man. Compared with its lithe young figure, Europe was actually in decrepitude. Mere class distinctions, the patois or dialect of the peasantry, the fixity of residence, the local costumes and habits marking a history that lost itself in the renewal of identical generations, raised from birth barriers which paralyzed half the population. Upon this mass of inert matter rested the church and state, holding down activity of thought.

This is not the dyspeptic Adams of the *Education* speaking, nor the man sneering at America in Hofstadter's description. The American man of a new order is just waiting for his chance to change the continent. Up to the year 1800, the Federalists had not given him that chance. We shall see in the work's final chapters how he was given the opportunity.

The Closing Chapters

One can hardly recognize in 1817 the America of 1800. The very face of the habitable territory has been drastically altered, first of all by a massive demographic displacement westward. In 1800 two thirds of the population lived within fifty miles of the Atlantic coast; only 10 percent lived west of the mountains. But the population of the three western states had quadrupled by 1817, and national expansion made necessary a national energy. Adams had predicted that much of this energy would be generated in the middle states, and so it turned out. New York and Pennsylvania were leading the way with canals, roads, and steamboat use. The financing of these and similar endeavors needed credit and banking systems to undergird them.

The formation of a professional military force called for systems of pay and pensions, supply and weaponry, ports and forts, logistics and accountability. Adams is proud and patriotic about the heroism of the navy all through the war and of the army by the end of it. In 1814 he could describe the fighting near Niagara this way: "For the fourth time in six weeks, a large body of British troops met a bloody and unparalleled check, if not rout, from an inferior force." A myth of our schoolbooks is that the American army won no real victories on land until Andrew Jackson's defense of New Orleans after the Treaty of Ghent had been signed. Adams exposes that for the nonsense it is.

The Jeffersonian years remade American politics. The old Federalists were discredited by their semi-treasonous actions in the War of 1812, and the Republicans were shocked out of the tropism toward France by Napoleon's quashing of the Revolution. What replaced these narrow ideologies was a new pragmatism, based on the territorial, economic, military, and technological demands placed on the expanding country. Thought was shaken out of its sectional compartments. It opened outward to science, experiment, cooperation, and technology. Patriotism shaped a national unity, while tolerance made it simultaneously more flexible, especially in religion.

The pulpits of New England, sloughing off a tired Calvinism, welcomed a whole new generation of Unitarians and Universalists. Energetic young preachers were called to major parishes—William Ellery Channing (twenty-three) in 1803, Joseph Stevens Buckminster (twenty-one) in 1805, Joseph Thatcher (twenty-five) in 1811. "No such display of fresh and winning genius had yet been seen in America as was offered by the genial outburst of intellectual activity in the early days of the Unitarian schism." The theological revolution won its great victory when a Unitarian, Henry Ware, was appointed to the chair of theology at Harvard. Humanism had thawed the icy regions of orthodoxy.

In history, a sense of national destiny replaced the doctrinal reading of events. In literature, romanticism replaced Augustanism and fed on American scenery to produce the early stages of Transcendentalism and the Hudson River School. William Cullen Bryant became what Whitman called him, "bard of the river and of the wood, ever conveying a taste of open air." Washington Irving gave a pawky twist to literature. Washington Alston brought painting back from Europe to make it American. The national ferment extended its effects throughout the entire culture.

This was not the result of planning on the Jeffersonians' part. In fact, Adams has the same sense of events that Tolstoy did in *War and Peace*, that events shape men, rather than men shaping events. In Tolstoy's image, the leaders are like hands on the face of a clock, thinking they move of themselves, while the hidden machinery is what drives them. But some men are more able to ride with the events (in Tolstoy's story it is Kutusov, not Napoleon, who intuits what the machinery is doing). In America, it was the Jeffersonians who were, willed-they nilled-they, on the side of history. That is clear from the state of America described in the first chapters, at the end of twelve years of Federalist rule, and the state described in the last chapters, after sixteen years of Republican rule. The Jeffersonians did not want war, but when it came they waged it, while the Federalists resisted it to the verge of treason (which Adams felt they crossed). When Republicans had to buy the West, they governed it, while Federalists resisted that. The Republicans formed a national party, which in turn formed national policies. They were so successful that Madison ended up his second term immensely popular, able to hand on the government to his logical successor, James Monroe. Adams did not extend his tale of the Virginia dynasty into that presidency, since he had a personal dislike for Monroe, as well as for his secretary of state—John Quincy Adams!

—GARRY WILLS

PART ONE

America in 1800

Physical and Economical Conditions

ACCORDING to the census of 1800, the United States of America contained 5,308,483 persons. In the same year the British Islands contained upwards of fifteen millions; the French Republic, more than twenty-seven millions. Nearly one fifth of the American people were negro slaves; the true political population consisted of four and a half million free whites, or less than one million able-bodied males, on whose shoulders fell the burden of a continent. Even after two centuries of struggle the land was still untamed; forest covered every portion, except here and there a strip of cultivated soil; the minerals lay undisturbed in their rocky beds, and more than two thirds of the people clung to the seaboard within fifty miles of tide-water, where alone the wants of civilized life could be supplied. The centre of population rested within eighteen miles of Baltimore, north and east of Washington. Except in political arrangement, the interior was little more civilized than in 1750, and was not much easier to penetrate than when La Salle and Hennepin found their way to the Mississippi more than a century before.

A great exception broke this rule. Two wagon-roads crossed the Alleghany Mountains in Pennsylvania,—one leading from Philadelphia to Pittsburg; one from the Potomac to the Monongahela; while a third passed through Virginia southwestward to the Holston River and Knoxville in Tennessee, with a branch through the Cumberland Gap into Kentucky. By these roads and by trails less passable from North and South Carolina, or by water-ways from the lakes, between four and five hundred thousand persons had invaded the country beyond the Alleghanies. At Pittsburg and on the Monongahela existed a society, already old, numbering seventy or eighty thousand persons, while on the Ohio River the settlements had grown to an importance which threatened to force a difficult problem on the union of the older States. One hundred and eighty thousand whites, with forty thousand negro slaves, made Kentucky the largest community west of the mountains; and about ninety thousand whites and fourteen thousand slaves were scattered over Tennessee. In the territory north of the Ohio less progress had been made. A New England colony existed at Marietta; some fifteen thousand people were gathered at Cincinnati; half-way between the two, a small town had grown up at Chillicothe, and other villages or straggling cabins were to be found elsewhere; but the whole Ohio territory contained only forty-five thousand inhabitants. The entire population, both free and slave, west of the mountains, reached not yet half a million; but already they were partly disposed to think themselves, and the old thirteen States were not altogether unwilling to consider them, the germ of an independent empire, which was to find its outlet, not through the Alleghanies to the seaboard, but by the Mississippi River to the Gulf.

Nowhere did eastern settlements touch the western. At least one hundred miles of mountainous country held the two regions everywhere apart. The shore of Lake Erie, where alone contact seemed easy, was still unsettled. The Indians had been pushed back to the Cuyahoga River, and a few cabins were built on the site of Cleveland; but in 1800, as in 1700, this intermediate region was only a portage where emigrants and merchandise were transferred from Lake Erie to the Muskingum and Ohio valleys. Even western New York remained a wilderness: Buffalo was not laid out; Indian titles were not extinguished; Rochester did not exist; and the county of Onondaga numbered a population of less than eight thousand. In 1799 Utica contained fifty houses, mostly small and temporary. Albany was still a Dutch city, with some five thousand inhabitants; and the tide of immigration flowed slowly through it into the valley of the Mohawk, while another stream from Pennsylvania, following the Susquehanna, spread toward the Genesee country.

The people of the old thirteen States, along the Atlantic seaboard, thus sent westward a wedge-shaped mass of nearly half a million persons, penetrating by the Tennessee, Cumberland, and Ohio rivers toward the western limit of the Union. The Indians offered sharp resistance to this invasion, exacting life for life, and yielding only as their warriors perished. By the close of the century the wedge of white settlements, with its apex at Nashville and its flanks covered by the Ohio and Tennessee rivers, nearly split the Indian country in halves. The northern half—consisting of the later States of Wisconsin, Michigan, Illinois, Indiana, and one third of Ohio—contained Wyandottes and Shawanese, Miamis, Kickapoos, and other tribes, able to send some five thousand warriors to hunt or fight. In the southern half, powerful confederacies of Creeks, Cherokees, Chickasaws, and Choctaws lived and hunted where the States of Mississippi, Alabama, and the western parts of Georgia, Tennessee, and Kentucky were to extend; and so weak was the State of Georgia, which claimed the southwestern territory for its own, that a well-concerted movement of Indians might without much difficulty have swept back its white population of one hundred thousand toward the ocean or across the Savannah River. The Indian power had been broken in halves, but each half was still terrible to the colonists on the edges of their vast domain, and was used as a political weapon by the Governments whose territory bounded the Union on the north and south. The governors-general of Canada intrigued with the northwestern Indians, that they might hold in check any aggression from Washington; while the Spanish governors of West Florida and Louisiana maintained equally close relations with the Indian confederacies of the Georgia territory.

With the exception that half a million people had crossed the Alleghanies and were struggling with difficulties all their own, in an isolation like that of Jutes or Angles in the fifth century, America, so far as concerned physical problems, had changed little in fifty years. The old landmarks remained nearly where they stood before. The same bad roads and difficult rivers, connecting the same small towns, stretched into the same forests in 1800 as when the armies of Braddock and Amherst pierced the western and northern wilderness, except that these roads extended a few miles farther from the seacoast. Nature was rather man's master than his servant, and the five million Americans struggling with the untamed continent seemed hardly more competent to their task than the beavers and buffalo which had for countless generations made bridges and roads of their own.

Even by water, along the seaboard, communication was as slow and almost as irregular as in colonial times. The wars in Europe caused a sudden and great increase in American shipping employed in foreign commerce, without yet leading to general improvement in navigation. The ordinary sea-going vessel carried a freight of about two hundred and fifty tons; the largest merchant ships hardly reached four hundred tons; the largest frigate in the United States navy, the "line-of-battle ship in disguise," had a capacity of fifteen hundred and seventy-six tons. Elaborately rigged as ships or brigs, the small merchant craft required large crews and were slow sailers; but the voyage to Europe was comparatively more comfortable and more regular than the voyage from New York to Albany, or through Long Island Sound to Providence. No regular packet plied between New York and Albany. Passengers waited till a sloop was advertised to sail; they provided their own bedding and supplies; and within the nineteenth century Captain Elias Bunker won much fame by building the sloop "Experiment," of one hundred and ten tons, to start regularly on a fixed day for Albany, for the convenience of passengers only, supplying beds, wine, and provisions for the voyage of one hundred and fifty miles. A week on the North River or on the Sound was an experience not at all unknown to travellers.

While little improvement had been made in water-travel, every increase of distance added to the difficulties of the westward journey. The settler who after buying wagon and horses hauled his family and goods across the mountains, might buy or build a broad flat-bottomed ark, to float with him and his fortunes down the Ohio, in constant peril of upsetting or of being sunk; but only light boats with strong oars could mount the stream, or boats forced against the current by laboriously poling in shallow water. If he carried his tobacco and wheat down the Mississippi to the Spanish port of New Orleans, and sold it, he might return to his home in Kentucky or Ohio by a long and dangerous journey on horseback through the Indian country from Natchez to Nashville, or he might take ship to Philadelphia, if a ship were about to sail, and again cross the Alleghanies. Compared with river travel, the sea was commonly an easy and safe highway. Nearly all the rivers which penetrated the interior were unsure, liable to be made dangerous by freshets, and both dangerous and impassable by drought; yet such as they were, these streams made the main paths of traffic. Through the mountainous gorges of the Susquehanna the produce of western New York first found an outlet; the Cuyahoga and Muskingum were the first highway from the Lakes to the Ohio; the Ohio itself, with its great tributaries the Cumberland and the Tennessee, marked the lines of western migration; and every stream which could at high water float a boat was thought likely to become a path for commerce. As General Washington, not twenty years earlier, hoped that the brawling waters of the Cheat and Youghiogheny might become the channel of trade between Chesapeake Bay and Pittsburg, so the Americans of 1800 were prepared to risk life and property on any streamlet that fell foaming down either flank of the Alleghanies. The experience of mankind proved trade to be dependent on water communications, and as yet Americans did not dream that the experience of mankind was useless to them.

If America was to be developed along the lines of water communication alone, by such means as were known to Europe, Nature had decided that the experiment of a single republican government must meet extreme difficulties. The valley of the Ohio had no more to do with that of the Hudson, the Susquehanna, the Potomac, the Roanoke, and the Santee, than the valley of the Danube with that of the Rhone, the Po, or the Elbe. Close communication by land could alone hold the great geographical divisions together either in interest or in fear. The union of New England with New York and Pennsylvania was not an easy task even as a problem of geography, and with an ocean highway; but the union of New England with the Carolinas, and of the seacoast with the interior, promised to be a hopeless undertaking. Physical contact alone could make one country of these isolated empires, but to the patriotic American of 1800, struggling for the continued existence of an embryo nation, with machinery so inadequate, the idea of ever bringing the Mississippi River, either by land or water, into close contact with New England, must have seemed wild. By water, an Erie Canal was already foreseen; by land, centuries of labor could alone conquer those obstacles which Nature permitted to be overcome.

In the minds of practical men, the experience of Europe left few doubts on this point. After two thousand years of public labor and private savings, even despotic monarchs, who employed the resources of their subjects as they pleased, could in

1800 pass from one part of their European dominions to another little more quickly than they might have done in the age
of the Antonines. A few short canals had been made, a few
bridges had been built, an excellent post-road extended from
Madrid to St. Petersburg; but the heavy diligence that rumbled
from Calais to Paris required three days for its journey of one
hundred and fifty miles, and if travellers ventured on a trip to
Marseilles they met with rough roads and hardships like those
of the Middle Ages. Italy was in 1800 almost as remote from the
north of Europe as when carriage-roads were first built. Neither
in time nor in thought was Florence or Rome much nearer to
London in Wordsworth's youth than in the youth of Milton or
Gray. Indeed, such changes as had occurred were partly for the
worse, owing to the violence of revolutionary wars during the
last ten years of the eighteenth century. Horace Walpole at his
life's close saw about him a world which in many respects was
less civilized than when as a boy he made the grand tour of
Europe.

While so little had been done on the great highways of
European travel, these highways were themselves luxuries
which furnished no sure measure of progress. The post-horses
toiled as painfully as ever through the sand from Hamburg to
Berlin, while the coach between York and London rolled along
an excellent road at the rate of ten miles an hour; yet neither in
England nor on the Continent was the post-road a great channel of commerce. No matter how good the road, it could not
compete with water, nor could heavy freights in great quantities be hauled long distances without extravagant cost. Water
communication was as necessary for European commerce in
1800 as it had been for the Phœnicians and Egyptians; the
Rhine, the Rhone, the Danube, the Elbe, were still the true
commercial highways, and except for government post-roads,
Europe was as dependent on these rivers in the eighteenth century as in the thirteenth. No certainty could be offered of more

rapid progress in the coming century than in the past; the chief hope seemed to lie in the construction of canals.

While Europe had thus consumed centuries in improving paths of trade, until merchandise could be brought by canal a few score miles from the Rhone to the Loire and Seine, to the Garonne and the Rhine, and while all her wealth and energy had not yet united the Danube with other river systems, America was required to construct, without delay, at least three great roads and canals, each several hundred miles long, across mountain ranges, through a country not yet inhabited, to points where no great markets existed,—and this under constant peril of losing her political union, which could not even by such connections be with certainty secured. After this should be accomplished, the Alleghanies must still remain between the eastern and western States, and at any known rate of travel Nashville could not be reached in less than a fortnight or three weeks from Philadelphia. Meanwhile the simpler problem of bringing New England nearer to Virginia and Georgia had not advanced even with the aid of a direct ocean highway. In becoming politically independent of England, the old thirteen provinces developed little more commercial intercourse with each other in proportion to their wealth and population than they had maintained in colonial days. The material ties that united them grew in strength no more rapidly than the ties which bound them to Europe. Each group of States lived a life apart.

Even the lightly equipped traveller found a short journey no slight effort. Between Boston and New York was a tolerable highway, along which, thrice a week, light stage-coaches carried passengers and the mail, in three days. From New York a stage-coach started every week-day for Philadelphia, consuming the greater part of two days in the journey; and the road between Paulus Hook, the modern Jersey City, and Hackensack, was declared by the newspapers in 1802 to be as bad as any other part of the route between Maine and Georgia. South of Philadelphia the road was tolerable as far as Baltimore, but between Baltimore and the new city of Washington it meandered through forests; the driver chose the track which seemed least dangerous, and rejoiced if in wet seasons he reached Washington without miring or upsetting his wagon. In the Northern States, four miles an hour was the average speed for any coach between Bangor and Baltimore. Beyond the Potomac the roads became steadily worse, until south of Petersburg even the mails were carried on horseback. Except for a stage-coach which plied between Charleston and Savannah, no public conveyance of any kind was mentioned in the three southernmost States.

The stage-coach was itself a rude conveyance, of a kind still familiar to experienced travellers. Twelve persons, crowded into one wagon, were jolted over rough roads, their bags and parcels, thrust inside, cramping their legs, while they were protected from the heat and dust of mid-summer and the intense cold and driving snow of winter only by leather flaps buttoned to the roof and sides. In fine, dry weather this mode of travel was not unpleasant, when compared with the heavy vehicles of Europe and the hard English turnpikes; but when spring rains drew the frost from the ground the roads became nearly impassable, and in winter, when the rivers froze, a serious peril was added, for the Susquehanna or the North River at Paulus Hook must be crossed in an open boat,—an affair of hours at best, sometimes leading to fatal accidents. Smaller annoyances of many kinds were habitual. The public, as a rule, grumbled less than might have been expected, but occasionally newspapers contained bitter complaints. An angry Philadelphian, probably a foreigner, wrote in 1796 that, "with a few exceptions, brutality, negligence, and filching are as naturally expected by people accustomed to travelling in America, as a mouth, a nose, and two eyes are looked for in a man's face." This sweeping charge, probably unjust, and certainly supported by little public evidence, was chiefly founded on the experience of an alleged journey from New York:—

> "At Bordentown we went into a second boat where we met with very sorry accommodation. This was about four o'clock in the afternoon. We had about twenty miles down the Delaware to reach Philadelphia. The captain, who had a most provoking tongue, was a boy about eighteen years of age. He and a few companions despatched a dozen or eighteen bottles of porter. We ran three different times against other vessels that were coming up the stream. The women and children lay all night on the bare boards of the cabin floor.... We reached Arch Street wharf about eight o'clock on the Wednesday morning, having been about sixteen hours on a voyage of twenty miles."

In the Southern States the difficulties and perils of travel were so great as to form a barrier almost insuperable. Even Virginia was no exception to this rule. At each interval of a few miles the horseman found himself stopped by a river, liable to sudden freshets, and rarely bridged. Jefferson in his frequent journeys between Monticello and Washington was happy to reach the end of the hundred miles without some vexatious delay. "Of eight rivers between here and Washington," he wrote to his Attorney-General in 1801, "five have neither bridges nor boats."

Expense caused an equally serious obstacle to travel. The usual charge in the Northern States was six cents a mile by stage. In the year 1796, according to Francis Baily, President of the Royal Astronomical Society, three or four stages ran daily from Baltimore to Philadelphia, the fare six dollars, with charges amounting to two dollars and a quarter a day at the inns on the road. Baily was three days in making the journey. From Philadelphia to New York he paid the same fare and charges, arriving in one day and a half. The entire journey of two hundred miles cost him twenty-one dollars. He remarked that travelling on the main lines of road in the settled country was about as expensive as in England, and when the roads were good, about as rapid. Congress allowed its members six dollars for every twenty miles travelled. The actual cost, including hotel expenses, could hardly have fallen below ten cents a mile.

Heavy traffic never used stage routes if it could find cheaper. Commerce between one State and another, or even between the seaboard and the interior of the same State, was scarcely possible on any large scale unless navigable water connected them. Except the great highway to Pittsburg, no road served as a channel of commerce between different regions of the country. In this respect New England east of the Connecticut was as independent of New York as both were independent of Virginia, and as Virginia in her turn was independent of Georgia and South Carolina. The chief value of inter-State communication by land rested in the postal system; but the post furnished another illustration of the difficulties which barred progress. In the year 1800 one general mail-route extended from Portland in Maine to Louisville in Georgia, the time required for the trip being twenty days. Between Portsmouth in New Hampshire and Petersburg in Virginia the contracts required a daily service, except Sundays; between Petersburg and Augusta the mail was carried thrice a week. Branching from the main line at New York, a mail went to Canandaigua in ten days; from Philadelphia another branch line went to Lexington in sixteen days, to Nashville in twenty-two days. Thus more than twenty thousand miles of post-road, with nine hundred post-offices, proved the vastness of the country and the smallness of the result; for the gross receipts for postage in the year ending Oct. 1, 1801, were only $320,000.

Throughout the land the eighteenth century ruled supreme. Only within a few years had the New Englander begun to abandon his struggle with a barren soil, among granite hills, to learn the comforts of easier existence in the valleys of the Mohawk and Ohio; yet the New England man was thought the shrewdest and most enterprising of Americans. If the Puritans and the Dutch needed a century or more to reach the Mohawk, when would they reach the Mississippi? The distance from New York to the Mississippi was about one thousand miles; from Washington to the extreme southwestern military post, below Natchez, was about twelve hundred. Scarcely a portion of western Europe was three hundred miles distant from some sea, but a width of three hundred miles was hardly more than an outskirt of the United States. No civilized country had yet been required to deal with physical difficulties so serious, nor did experience warrant conviction that such difficulties could be overcome.

If the physical task which lay before the American people had advanced but a short way toward completion, little more change could be seen in the economical conditions of American life. The man who in the year 1800 ventured to hope for a new era in the coming century, could lay his hand on no statistics that silenced doubt. The machinery of production showed no radical difference from that familiar to ages long past. The Saxon farmer of the eighth century enjoyed most of the comforts known to Saxon farmers of the eighteenth. The eorls and ceorls of Offa and Ecgbert could not read or write, and did not receive a weekly newspaper with such information as newspapers in that age could supply; yet neither their houses, their clothing, their food and drink, their agricultural tools and methods, their stock, nor their habits were so greatly altered or improved by time that they would have found much difficulty in accommodating their lives to that of their descendants in the eighteenth century. In this respect America was backward. Fifty or a hundred miles inland more than half the houses were log-cabins, which might or might not enjoy the luxury of a glass window. Throughout the South and West houses showed little attempt at luxury; but even in New England the ordinary farm-house was hardly so well built, so spacious, or so warm as that of a well-to-do contemporary of Charlemagne. The cloth which the farmer's family wore was still homespun. The hats were manufactured by the village hatter; the clothes were cut and made at home; the shirts, socks, and nearly every other article of dress were also home-made. Hence came a marked air of rus-ticity which distinguished country from town,—awkward shapes of hat, coat, and trousers, which gave to the Yankee car-icature those typical traits that soon disappeared almost as completely as coats of mail and steel head-pieces. The plough was rude and clumsy; the sickle as old as Tubal Cain, and even the cradle not in general use; the flail was unchanged since the Aryan exodus; in Virginia, grain was still commonly trodden out by horses. Enterprising gentlemen-farmers introduced threshing-machines and invented scientific ploughs; but these were novelties. Stock was as a rule not only unimproved, but ill cared for. The swine ran loose; the cattle were left to feed on what pasture they could find, and even in New England were not housed until the severest frosts, on the excuse that exposure hardened them. Near half a century afterward a competent judge asserted that the general treatment of cows in New Eng-land was fair matter of presentment by a grand jury. Except among the best farmers, drainage, manures, and rotation of crops were uncommon. The ordinary cultivator planted his corn as his father had planted it, sowing as much rye to the acre, using the same number of oxen to plough, and getting in his crops on the same day. He was even known to remove his barn on account of the manure accumulated round it, although the New England soil was never so rich as to warrant neglect to enrich it. The money for which he sold his wheat and chickens was of the Old World; he reckoned in shillings or pistareens, and rarely handled an American coin more valuable than a large copper cent.

At a time when the wealth and science of London and Paris could not supply an article so necessary as a common sulphur-match, the backwardness of remote country districts could hardly be exaggerated. Yet remote districts were not the only sufferers. Of the whole United States New England claimed to be the most civilized province, yet New England was a region in which life had yet gained few charms of sense and few advantages over its rivals. Wilson, the ornithologist, a Pennsylvania Scotchman, a confirmed grumbler, but a shrewd judge, and the most thorough of American travellers, said in 1808: "My journey through almost the whole of New England has rather lowered the Yankees in my esteem. Except a few neat academies, I found their schoolhouses equally ruinous and deserted with ours; fields covered with stones; stone fences; scrubby oaks and pine-trees; wretched orchards; scarcely one grain-field in twenty miles; the taverns along the road dirty, and filled with loungers brawling about lawsuits and politics; the people snappish and extortioners, lazy, and two hundred years behind the Pennsylvanians in agricultural improvements." The description was exaggerated, for Wilson forgot to speak of the districts where fields were not covered with stones, and where wheat could be grown to advantage. Twenty years earlier, Albert Gallatin, who knew Pennsylvania well, having reached Hartford on his way to Boston, wrote: "I have seen nothing in America equal to the establishments on the Connecticut River." Yet Wilson's account described the first general effect of districts in the New England States, where agriculture was backward and the country poor. The houses were thin wooden buildings, not well suited to the climate; the churches were unwarmed; the clothing was poor; sanitary laws were few, and a bathroom or a soil-pipe was unknown. Consumption, typhoid, scarlet fever, diphtheria, and rheumatic fevers were common; habits of drinking were still a scourge in every family, and dyspepsia destroyed more victims than were consumed by drink. Population increased slowly, as though the conditions of life were more than usually hard. A century earlier, Massachusetts was supposed to contain sixty thousand inhabitants. Governor Hutchinson complained that while the other colonies quadrupled their numbers, Massachusetts failed to double its population in fifty years. In 1790 the State contained 378,000 people, not including the province of Maine; in 1800 the number rose to 423,000, which showed that a period of more rapid growth had begun, for the emigration into other States was also large.

A better measure of the difficulties with which New England struggled was given by the progress of Boston, which was supposed to have contained about eighteen thousand inhabitants as early as 1730, and twenty thousand in 1770. For several years after the Revolution it numbered less than twenty thousand, but in 1800 the census showed twenty-five thousand inhabitants. In appearance, Boston resembled an English market-town, of a kind even then old-fashioned. The footways or sidewalks were paved, like the crooked and narrow streets, with round cobblestones, and were divided from the carriage way only by posts and a gutter. The streets were almost unlighted at night, a few oil-lamps rendering the darkness more visible and the rough pavement rougher. Police hardly existed. The system of taxation was defective. The town was managed by selectmen, the elected instruments of town-meetings whose jealousy of granting power was even greater than their objection to spending money, and whose hostility to city government was not to be overcome.

Although on all sides increase of ease and comfort was evident, and roads, canals, and new buildings, public and private, were already in course of construction on a scale before unknown, yet in spite of more than a century and a half of incessant industry, intelligent labor, and pinching economy Boston and New England were still poor. A few merchants enjoyed incomes derived from foreign trade, which allowed them to imitate in a quiet way the style of the English mercantile class; but the clergy and the lawyers, who stood at the head of society, lived with much economy. Many a country clergyman, eminent for piety and even for hospitality, brought up a family and laid aside some savings on a salary of five hundred dollars a year. President Dwight, who knew well the class to which he belonged, eulogizing the life of Abijah Weld, pastor of Attleborough, declared that on a salary of two hundred and twenty dollars a year Mr. Weld brought up eleven children, besides keeping a hospitable house and maintaining charity to the poor.

On the Exchange a few merchants had done most of the business of Boston since the peace of 1783, but six mailcoaches a week to New York, and occasional arrivals from Europe, or the departure of a ship to China, left ample leisure for correspondence and even for gossip. The habits of the commercial class had not been greatly affected by recent prosperity. Within ten or fifteen years before 1800 three Banks had been created to supply the commercial needs of Boston. One of these was a branch Bank of the United States, which employed there whatever part of its capital it could profitably use; the two others were local Banks, with capital of $1,600,000, toward which the State subscribed $400,000. Altogether the banking capital of Boston might amount to two millions and a half. A number of small Banks, representing in all about two and a half millions more, were scattered through the smaller New England towns. The extraordinary prosperity caused by the French wars opened to Boston a new career. Wealth and population were doubling; the exports and imports of New England were surprisingly large, and the shipping was greater than that of New York and Pennsylvania combined; but Boston had already learned, and was to learn again, how fleeting were the riches that depended on foreign commerce, and conservative habits were not easily changed by a few years of accidental gain.

Of manufactures New England had many, but none on a large scale. The people could feed or clothe themselves only by household industry; their whale-oil, salt fish, lumber, and rum were mostly sent abroad; but they freighted coasters with turners' articles, home-made linens and cloths, cheese, butter, shoes, nails, and what were called Yankee Notions of all sorts, which were sent to Norfolk and the Southern ports, and often peddled from the deck, as goods of every sort were peddled on the flat-boats of the Ohio. Two or three small mills spun cotton with doubtful success; but England supplied ordinary manufactures more cheaply and better than Massachusetts could hope to do. A tri-weekly mail and a few coasting sloops provided for the business of New England with domestic ports. One packet sloop plied regularly to New York.

The State of New York was little in advance of Massachusetts and Maine. In 1800 for the first time New York gained the lead in population by the difference between 589,000 and 573,000. The valuation of New York for the direct tax in 1799 was $100,000,000; that of Massachusetts was $84,000,000. New York was still a frontier State, and although the city was European in its age and habits, travellers needed to go few miles from the Hudson in order to find a wilderness like that of Ohio and Tennessee. In most material respects the State was behind New England; outside the city was to be seen less wealth and less appearance of comfort. The first impression commonly received of any new country was from its inns, and on the whole few better tests of material condition then existed. President Dwight, though maintaining that the best old-fashioned inns of New England were in their way perfect, being in fact excellent private houses, could not wholly approve what he called the modern inns, even in Connecticut; but when he passed into New York he asserted that everything suffered an instant change for the worse. He explained that in Massachusetts the authorities were strict in refusing licenses to any but respectable and responsible persons, whereas in New York licenses were granted to any one who would pay for them, —which caused a multiplication of dram-shops, bad accommodations, and a gathering of loafers and tipplers about every tavern porch, whose rude appearance, clownish manners, drunkenness, swearing, and obscenity confirmed the chief of Federalist clergymen in his belief that democracy had an evil influence on morals.

Far more movement was to be seen, and accumulation was more rapid than in colonial days; but little had yet been done for improvement, either by Government or by individuals, beyond some provision for extending roads and clearing watercourses behind the advancing settlers. If Washington Irving was right, Rip Van Winkle, who woke from his long slumber about the year 1800, saw little that was new to him, except the head of President Washington where that of King George had once hung, and strange faces instead of familiar ones. Except in numbers, the city was relatively no farther advanced than the country. Between 1790 and 1800 its population rose from 33,000 to 60,000; and if Boston resembled an old-fashioned English market-town, New York was like a foreign seaport, badly paved, undrained, and as foul as a town surrounded by the tides could be. Although the Manhattan Company was laying wooden pipes for a water supply, no sanitary regulations were enforced, and every few years—as in 1798 and 1803—yellow fever swept away crowds of victims, and drove the rest of the population, panic stricken, into the highlands. No day-police existed; constables were still officers of the courts; the night-police consisted of two captains, two deputies, and seventy-two men. The estimate for the city's expenses in 1800 amounted to $130,000. One marked advantage New York enjoyed over Boston, in the possession of a city government able to introduce reforms. Thus, although still mediæval in regard to drainage and cleanliness, the town had taken advantage of recurring fires to rebuild some of the streets with brick sidewalks and curbstones. Travellers dwelt much on this improvement, which only New York and Philadelphia had yet adopted, and Europeans agreed that both had the air of true cities: that while Boston was the Bristol of America, New York was the Liverpool, and Philadelphia the London.

In respect to trade and capital, New York possessed growing advantages, supplying half New Jersey and Connecticut, a part of Massachusetts, and all the rapidly increasing settlements on the branches of the Hudson; but no great amount of wealth, no considerable industry or new creation of power was yet to be seen. Two Banks, besides the branch Bank of the United States, supplied the business wants of the city, and employed about the same amount of capital in loans and discounts as was required for Boston. Besides these city institutions but two other Banks existed in the State,—at Hudson and at Albany.

The proportion of capital in private hands seemed to be no larger. The value of exports from New York in 1800 was but $14,000,000; the net revenue on imports for 1799 was $2,373,000, against $1,607,000 collected in Massachusetts. Such a foreign trade required little capital, yet these values represented a great proportion of all the exchanges. Domestic manufactures could not compete with foreign, and employed little bank credit. Speculation was slow, mostly confined to lands which required patience to exchange or sell. The most important undertakings were turnpikes, bridges such as Boston built across the Charles, or new blocks of houses; and a canal, such as Boston designed to the Merrimac, overstrained the resources of capital. The entire banking means of the United States in 1800 would not have answered the stock-jobbing purposes of one great operator of Wall Street in 1875. The nominal capital of all the Banks, including the Bank of the United

States, fell short of $29,000,000. The limit of credit was quickly reached, for only the richest could borrow more than fifteen or twenty thousand dollars at a time, and the United States Government itself was gravely embarrassed whenever obliged to raise money. In 1798 the Secretary of the Treasury could obtain five million dollars only by paying eight per cent interest for a term of years; and in 1814 the Government was forced to stop payments for the want of twenty millions.

The precise value of American trade was uncertain, but in 1800 the gross exports and imports of the United States may have balanced at about seventy-five million dollars. The actual consumption of foreign merchandise amounted perhaps to the value of forty or fifty million dollars, paid in wheat, cotton, and other staples, and by the profits on the shipping employed in carrying West India produce to Europe. The amount of American capital involved in a trade of fifty millions, with credits of three, six, and nine months, must have been small, and the rates of profit large.

As a rule American capital was absorbed in shipping or agriculture, whence it could not be suddenly withdrawn. No stock-exchange existed, and no broker exclusively engaged in stock-jobbing, for there were few stocks. The national debt, of about eighty millions, was held abroad, or as a permanent investment at home. States and municipalities had not learned to borrow. Except for a few banks and insurance offices, turnpikes, bridges, canals, and land-companies, neither bonds nor stocks were known. The city of New York was so small as to make extravagance difficult; the Battery was a fashionable walk, Broadway a country drive, and Wall Street an uptown residence. Great accumulations of wealth had hardly begun. The Patroon was still the richest man in the State. John Jacob Astor was a fur-merchant living where the Astor House afterward stood, and had not yet begun those purchases of real estate which secured his fortune. Cornelius Vanderbilt was a boy six years old, playing about his father's ferry-boat at Staten Island. New York city itself was what it had been for a hundred years past,—a local market.

As a national capital New York made no claim to consideration. If Bostonians for a moment forgot their town-meetings, or if Virginians overcame their dislike for cities and pavements, they visited and admired, not New York, but Philadelphia. "Philadelphia," wrote the Duc de Liancourt, "is not only the finest city in the United States, but may be deemed one of the most beautiful cities in the world." In truth, it surpassed any of its size on either side of the Atlantic for most of the comforts and some of the elegancies of life. While Boston contained twenty-five thousand inhabitants and New York sixty thousand, the census of 1800 showed that Philadelphia was about the size of Liverpool,—a city of seventy thousand people. The repeated ravages of yellow fever roused there a regard for sanitary precautions and cleanliness; the city, well paved and partly drained, was supplied with water in wooden pipes, and was the best-lighted town in America; its market was a model, and its jail was intended also for a model,—although the first experiment proved unsuccessful, because the prisoners went mad or idiotic in solitary confinement. In and about the city flourished industries considerable for the time. The iron-works were already important; paper and gunpowder, pleasure carriages and many other manufactures, were produced on a larger scale than elsewhere in the Union. Philadelphia held the seat of government until July, 1800, and continued to hold the Bank of the United States, with its capital of ten millions, besides private banking capital to the amount of five millions more. Public spirit was more active in Pennsylvania than in New York. More roads and canals were building; a new turnpike ran from Philadelphia to Lancaster, and the great highway to Pittsburg was a more important artery of national life than was controlled by any other State. The exports of Pennsylvania amounted to

$12,000,000, and the custom-house produced $1,350,000. The State contained six hundred thousand inhabitants,—a population somewhat larger than that of New York.

Of all parts of the Union, Pennsylvania seemed to have made most use of her national advantages; but her progress was not more rapid than the natural increase of population and wealth demanded, while to deal with the needs of America, man's resources and his power over Nature must be increased in a ratio far more rapid than that which governed his numbers. Nevertheless, Pennsylvania was the most encouraging spectacle in the field of vision. Baltimore, which had suddenly sprung to a population and commerce greater than those of Boston, also offered strong hope of future improvement; but farther South the people showed fewer signs of change.

The city of Washington, rising in a solitude on the banks of the Potomac, was a symbol of American nationality in the Southern States. The contrast between the immensity of the task and the paucity of means seemed to challenge suspicion that the nation itself was a magnificent scheme like the federal city, which could show only a few log-cabins and negro quarters where the plan provided for the traffic of London and the elegance of Versailles. When in the summer of 1800 the government was transferred to what was regarded by most persons as a fever-stricken morass, the half-finished White House stood in a naked field overlooking the Potomac, with two awkward Department buildings near it, a single row of brick houses and a few isolated dwellings within sight, and nothing more; until across a swamp, a mile and a half away, the shapeless, unfinished Capitol was seen, two wings without a body, ambitious enough in design to make more grotesque the nature of its surroundings. The conception proved that the United States understood the vastness of their task, and were willing to stake something on their faith in it. Never did hermit or saint condemn himself to solitude more consciously than Congress and the Executive in removing the government from Philadelphia to Washington: the discontented men clustered together in eight or ten boarding-houses as near as possible to the Capitol, and there lived, like a convent of monks, with no other amusement or occupation than that of going from their lodgings to the Chambers and back again. Even private wealth could do little to improve their situation, for there was nothing which wealth could buy; there were in Washington no shops or markets, skilled labor, commerce, or people. Public efforts and lavish use of public money could alone make the place tolerable; but Congress doled out funds for this national and personal object with so sparing a hand, that their Capitol threatened to crumble in pieces and crush Senate and House under the ruins, long before the building was complete.

A government capable of sketching a magnificent plan, and willing to give only a half-hearted pledge for its fulfilment; a people eager to advertise a vast undertaking beyond their present powers, which when completed would become an object of jealousy and fear,—this was the impression made upon the traveller who visited Washington in 1800, and mused among the unraised columns of the Capitol upon the destiny of the United States. As he travelled farther south his doubts were strengthened, for across the Potomac he could detect no sign of a new spirit. Manufactures had no existence. Alexandria owned a bank with half a million of capital, but no other was to be found between Washington and Charleston, except the branch Bank of the United States at Norfolk, nor any industry to which loans and discounts could safely be made. Virginia, the most populous and powerful of all the States, had a white population of 514,000, nearly equal to that of Pennsylvania and New York, besides about 350,000 slaves. Her energies had pierced the mountains and settled the western territory before the slow-moving Northern people had torn themselves from the safer and more comfortable life by the seaboard; but the

Virginia ideal was patriarchal, and an American continent on the Virginia type might reproduce the virtues of Cato, and perhaps the eloquence of Cicero, but was little likely to produce anything more practical in the way of modern progress. The Shenandoah Valley rivalled Pennsylvania and Connecticut in richness and skill of husbandry; but even agriculture, the favorite industry in Virginia, had suffered from the competition of Kentucky and Tennessee, and from the emigration which had drawn away fully one hundred thousand people. The land was no longer very productive. Even Jefferson, the most active-minded and sanguine of all Virginians,—the inventor of the first scientific plough, the importer of the first threshing-machine known in Virginia, the experimenter with a new drilling-machine, the owner of one hundred and fifty slaves and ten thousand acres of land, whose negroes were trained to carpentry, cabinet-making, house-building, weaving, tailoring, shoemaking,—claimed to get from his land no more than six or eight bushels of wheat to an acre, and had been forced to abandon the more profitable cultivation of tobacco. Except in a few favored districts like the Shenandoah Valley, land in Virginia did not average eight bushels of wheat to an acre. The cultivation of tobacco had been almost the sole object of land-owners, and even where the lands were not exhausted, a bad system of agriculture and the force of habit prevented improvement.

The great planters lavished money in vain on experiments to improve their crops and their stock. They devoted themselves to the task with energy and knowledge; but they needed a diversity of interests and local markets, and except at Baltimore these were far from making their appearance. Neither the products, the markets, the relative amount of capital, nor the machinery of production had perceptibly changed. "The Virginians are not generally rich," said the Duc de Liancourt, "especially in net revenue. Thus one often finds a well-served table, covered with silver, in a room where for ten years half the window panes have been missing, and where they will be missed for ten years more. There are few houses in a passable state of repair, and of all parts of the establishment those best cared for are the stables." Wealth reckoned in slaves or land was plenty; but the best Virginians, from President Washington downward, were most outspoken in their warnings against the Virginia system both of slavery and agriculture.

The contrast between Virginia and Pennsylvania was the subject of incessant comment.

"In Pennsylvania," said Robert Sutcliffe, an English Friend who published travels made in 1804–1806, "we meet great numbers of wagons drawn by four or more fine fat horses, the carriages firm and well made, and covered with stout good linen, bleached almost white; and it is not uncommon to see ten or fifteen together travelling cheerfully along the road, the driver riding on one of his horses. Many of these come more than three hundred miles to Philadelphia from the Ohio, Pittsburg, and other places, and I have been told by a respectable Friend, a native of Philadelphia, that more than one thousand covered carriages frequently come to Philadelphia market.... The appearance of things in the Slave States is quite the reverse of this. We sometimes meet a ragged black boy or girl driving a team consisting of a lean cow and a mule; sometimes a lean bull or an ox and a mule; and I have seen a mule, a bull, and a cow each miserable in its appearance, composing one team, with a half-naked black slave or two riding or driving as occasion suited. The carriage or wagon, if it may be called such, appeared in as wretched a condition as the team and its driver. Sometimes a couple of horses, mules, or cows would be dragging a hogshead of tobacco, with a pivot or axle driven into each end of the hogshead, and something like

a shaft attached, by which it was drawn or rolled along
the road. I have seen two oxen and two slaves pretty fully
employed in getting along a single hogshead; and some of
these come from a great distance inland."

In the middle of these primitive sights, Sutcliffe was startled
by a contrast such as Virginia could always show. Between
Richmond and Fredericksburg,—

"In the afternoon, as our road lay through the woods, I
was surprised to meet a family party travelling along in as
elegant a coach as is usually met with in the neighborhood of London, and attended by several gayly dressed
footmen."

The country south of Virginia seemed unpromising even to
Virginians. In the year 1796 President Washington gave to Sir
John Sinclair his opinion upon the relative value of American
lands. He then thought the valley of Virginia the garden of
America; but he would say nothing to induce others to settle in
more southern regions.

"The uplands of North and South Carolina and Georgia
are not dissimilar in soil," he wrote, "but as they approach the lower latitudes are less congenial to wheat,
and are supposed to be proportionably more unhealthy.
Towards the seaboard of all the Southern States, and farther south more so, the lands are low, sandy, and unhealthy; for which reason I shall say little concerning
them, for as I should not choose to be an inhabitant of
them myself, I ought not to say anything that would induce others to be so. . . . I understand that from thirty to
forty dollars per acre may be denominated the medium
price in the vicinity of the Susquehanna in the State of

Pennsylvania, from twenty to thirty on the Potomac in what is called the Valley, . . . and less, as I have noticed before, as you proceed southerly."

Whatever was the cause, the State of North Carolina seemed to offer few temptations to immigrants or capital. Even in white population ranking fifth among the sixteen States, her 478,000 inhabitants were unknown to the world. The beautiful upper country attracted travellers neither for pleasure nor for gain, while the country along the sea-coast was avoided except by hardy wanderers. The grumbling Wilson, who knew every nook and corner of the United States, and who found New England so dreary, painted this part of North Carolina in colors compared with which his sketch of New England was gay. "The taverns are the most desolate and beggarly imaginable; bare, bleak, and dirty walls, one or two old broken chairs and a bench form all the furniture. The white females seldom make their appearance. At supper you sit down to a meal the very sight of which is sufficient to deaden the most eager appetite, and you are surrounded by half-a-dozen dirty, half-naked blacks, male and female, whom any man of common scent might smell a quarter of a mile off. The house itself is raised upon props four or five feet, and the space below is left open for the hogs, with whose charming vocal performance the wearied traveller is serenaded the whole night long." The landscape pleased him no better,—"immense solitary pine savannahs through which the road winds among stagnant ponds; dark, sluggish creeks of the color of brandy, over which are thrown high wooden bridges without railings," crazy and rotten.

North Carolina was relatively among the poorest States. The exports and imports were of trifling value, less than one tenth of those returned for Massachusetts, which were more than twice as great as those of North Carolina and Virginia together. That under these conditions America should receive any strong impulse from such a quarter seemed unlikely; yet perhaps for the moment more was to be expected from the Carolinas than from Virginia. Backward as these States in some respects were, they possessed one new element of wealth which promised more for them than anything Virginia could hope. The steam-engines of Watt had been applied in England to spinning, weaving, and printing cotton; an immense demand had risen for that staple, and the cotton-gin had been simultaneously invented. A sudden impetus was given to industry; land which had been worthless and estates which had become bankrupt acquired new value, and in 1800 every planter was growing cotton, buying negroes, and breaking fresh soil. North Carolina felt the strong flood of prosperity, but South Carolina, and particularly the town of Charleston, had most to hope. The exports of South Carolina were nearly equal in value to those of Massachusetts or Pennsylvania; the imports were equally large. Charleston might reasonably expect to rival Boston, New York, Philadelphia, and Baltimore. In 1800 these cities still stood, as far as concerned their foreign trade, within some range of comparison; and between Boston, Baltimore, and Charleston, many plausible reasons could be given for thinking that the last might have the most brilliant future. The three towns stood abreast. If Charleston had but about eighteen thousand inhabitants, this was the number reported by Boston only ten years before, and was five thousand more than Baltimore then boasted. Neither Boston nor Baltimore saw about them a vaster region to supply, or so profitable a staple to export. A cotton crop of two hundred thousand pounds sent abroad in 1791 grew to twenty millions in 1801, and was to double again by 1803. An export of fifty thousand bales was enormous, yet was only the beginning. What use might not Charleston, the only considerable town in the entire South, make of this golden flood?

The town promised hopefully to prove equal to its task.

Nowhere in the Union was intelligence, wealth, and education greater in proportion to numbers than in the little society of cotton and rice planters who ruled South Carolina; and they were in 1800 not behind—they hoped soon to outstrip—their rivals. If Boston was building a canal to the Merrimac, and Philadelphia one along the Schuylkill to the Susquehanna, Charleston had nearly completed another which brought the Santee River to its harbor, and was planning a road to Tennessee which should draw the whole interior within reach. Nashville was nearer to Charleston than to any other seaport of the Union, and Charleston lay nearest to the rich trade of the West Indies. Not even New York seemed more clearly marked for prosperity than this solitary Southern city, which already possessed banking capital in abundance, intelligence, enterprise, the traditions of high culture and aristocratic ambition, all supported by slave-labor, which could be indefinitely increased by the African slave-trade.

If any portion of the United States might hope for a sudden and magnificent bloom, South Carolina seemed entitled to expect it. Rarely had such a situation, combined with such resources, failed to produce some wonderful result. Yet as Washington warned Sinclair, these advantages were counterbalanced by serious evils. The climate in summer was too relaxing. The sun was too hot. The sea-coast was unhealthy, and at certain seasons even deadly to the whites. Finally, if history was a guide, no permanent success could be prophesied for a society like that of the low country in South Carolina, where some thirty thousand whites were surrounded by a dense mass of nearly one hundred thousand negro slaves. Even Georgia, then only partially settled, contained sixty thousand slaves and but one hundred thousand whites. The cotton States might still argue that if slavery, malaria, or summer heat barred civilization, all the civilization that was ever known must have been blighted in its infancy; but although the future of South

Carolina might be brilliant, like that of other oligarchies in which only a few thousand freemen took part, such a development seemed to diverge far from the path likely to be followed by Northern society, and bade fair to increase and complicate the social and economical difficulties with which Americans had to deal.

A probable valuation of the whole United States in 1800 was eighteen hundred million dollars, equal to $328 for each human being, including slaves; or $418 to each free white. This property was distributed with an approach to equality, except in a few of the Southern States. In New York and Philadelphia a private fortune of one hundred thousand dollars was considered handsome, and three hundred thousand was great wealth. Inequalities were frequent; but they were chiefly those of a landed aristocracy. Equality was so far the rule that every white family of five persons might be supposed to own land, stock, or utensils, a house and furniture, worth about two thousand dollars; and as the only considerable industry was agriculture, their scale of life was easy to calculate,—taxes amounting to little or nothing, and wages averaging about a dollar a day.

Not only were these slender resources, but they were also of a kind not easily converted to the ready uses required for rapid development. Among the numerous difficulties with which the Union was to struggle, and which were to form the interest of American history, the disproportion between the physical obstacles and the material means for overcoming them was one of the most striking.

Popular Characteristics

THE GROWTH of character, social and national,—the formation of men's minds,—more interesting than any territorial or industrial growth, defied the tests of censuses and surveys. No people could be expected, least of all when in infancy, to understand the intricacies of its own character, and rarely has a foreigner been gifted with insight to explain what natives did not comprehend. Only with diffidence could the best-informed Americans venture, in 1800, to generalize on the subject of their own national habits of life and thought. Of all American travellers President Dwight was the most experienced; yet his four volumes of travels were remarkable for no trait more uniform than their reticence in regard to the United States. Clear and emphatic wherever New England was in discussion, Dwight claimed no knowledge of other regions. Where so good a judge professed ignorance, other observers were likely to mislead; and Frenchmen like Liancourt, Englishmen like Weld, or Germans like Bülow, were almost equally worthless authorities on a subject which none understood. The newspapers of the time were little more trustworthy than the books of travel, and hardly so well written. The literature of a higher kind was chiefly limited to New England, New York, and Pennsylvania. From materials so poor no precision of result could be expected. A few customs, more or less local; a few prejudices, more or less popular; a few traits of thought, suggesting habits of mind,—must form the entire material for a study more important than that of politics or economics.

The standard of comfort had much to do with the standard of character; and in the United States, except among the slaves, the laboring class enjoyed an ample supply of the necessaries of life. In this respect, as in some others, they claimed superiority over the laboring class in Europe, and the claim would have been still stronger had they shown more skill in using the abundance that surrounded them. The Duc de Liancourt, among foreigners the best and kindest observer, made this remark on the mode of life he saw in Pennsylvania:—

> "There is a contrast of cleanliness with its opposite which to a stranger is very remarkable. The people of the country are as astonished that one should object to sleeping two or three in the same bed and in dirty sheets, or to drink from the same dirty glass after half a score of others, as to see one neglect to wash one's hands and face of a morning. Whiskey diluted with water is the ordinary country drink. There is no settler, however poor, whose family does not take coffee or chocolate for breakfast, and always a little salt meat; at dinner, salt meat, or salt fish, and eggs; at supper again salt meat and coffee. This is also the common regime of the taverns."

An amusing, though quite untrustworthy Englishman named Ashe, who invented an American journey in 1806, described the fare of a Kentucky cabin:—

> "The dinner consisted of a large piece of salt bacon, a dish of hominy, and a tureen of squirrel broth. I dined entirely on the last dish, which I found incomparably good, and the meat equal to the most delicate chicken. The Kentuckian eat nothing but bacon, which indeed is

the favorite diet of all the inhabitants of the State, and drank nothing but whiskey, which soon made him more than two-thirds drunk. In this last practice he is also supported by the public habit. In a country, then, where bacon and spirits form the favorite summer repast, it cannot be just to attribute entirely the causes of infirmity to the climate. No people on earth live with less regard to regimen. They eat salt meat three times a day, seldom or never have any vegetables, and drink ardent spirits from morning till night. They have not only an aversion to fresh meat, but a vulgar prejudice that it is unwholesome. The truth is, their stomachs are depraved by burning liquors, and they have no appetite for anything but what is high-flavored and strongly impregnated by salt."

Salt pork three times a day was regarded as an essential part of American diet. In the "Chainbearer," Cooper described what he called American poverty as it existed in 1784. "As for bread," said the mother, "I count that for nothing. We always have bread and potatoes enough; but I hold a family to be in a desperate way when the mother can see the bottom of the pork-barrel. Give me the children that's raised on good sound pork afore all the game in the country. Game's good as a relish, and so's bread; but pork is the staff of life . . . My children I calkerlate to bring up on pork."

Many years before the time to which Cooper referred, Poor Richard asked: "Maids of America, who gave you bad teeth?" and supplied the answer: "Hot soupings and frozen apples." Franklin's question and answer were repeated in a wider sense by many writers, but none was so emphatic as Volney:—

"I will venture to say," declared Volney, "that if a prize were proposed for the scheme of a regimen most calculated to injure the stomach, the teeth, and the health in general, no better could be invented than that of the Americans. In the morning at breakfast they deluge their stomach with a quart of hot water, impregnated with tea, or so slightly with coffee that it is mere colored water; and they swallow, almost without chewing, hot bread, half baked, toast soaked in butter, cheese of the fattest kind, slices of salt or hung beef, ham, etc., all which are nearly insoluble. At dinner they have boiled pastes under the name of puddings, and the fattest are esteemed the most delicious; all their sauces, even for roast beef, are melted butter; their turnips and potatoes swim in hog's lard, butter, or fat; under the name of pie or pumpkin, their pastry is nothing but a greasy paste, never sufficiently baked. To digest these viscous substances they take tea almost instantly after dinner, making it so strong that it is absolutely bitter to the taste, in which state it affects the nerves so powerfully that even the English find it brings on a more obstinate restlessness than coffee. Supper again introduces salt meats or oysters. As Chastellux says, the whole day passes in heaping indigestions on one another; and to give tone to the poor, relaxed, and wearied stomach, they drink Madeira, rum, French brandy, gin, or malt spirits, which complete the ruin of the nervous system."

An American breakfast never failed to interest foreigners, on account of the variety and abundance of its dishes. On the main lines of travel, fresh meat and vegetables were invariably served at all meals; but Indian corn was the national crop, and Indian corn was eaten three times a day in another form as salt pork. The rich alone could afford fresh meat. Ice-chests were hardly known. In the country fresh meat could not regularly be got, except in the shape of poultry or game; but the hog cost nothing to keep, and very little to kill and preserve. Thus the ordinary rural American was brought up on salt pork and Indian corn, or rye; and the effect of this diet showed itself in dyspepsia.

One of the traits to which Liancourt alluded marked more distinctly the stage of social development. By day or by night, privacy was out of the question. Not only must all men travel in the same coach, dine at the same table, at the same time, on the same fare, but even their beds were in common, without distinction of persons. Innkeepers would not understand that a different arrangement was possible. When the English traveller Weld reached Elkton, on the main road from Philadelphia to Baltimore, he asked the landlord what accommodation he had. "Don't trouble yourself about that," was the reply; "I have no less than eleven beds in one room alone." This primitive habit extended over the whole country from Massachusetts to Georgia, and no American seemed to revolt against the tyranny of innkeepers.

"At New York I was lodged with two others, in a back room on the ground floor," wrote, in 1796, the Philadelphian whose complaints have already been mentioned. "What can be the reason for that vulgar, hoggish custom, common in America, of squeezing three, six, or eight beds into one room?"

Nevertheless, the Americans were on the whole more neat than their critics allowed. "You have not seen the Americans," was Cobbett's reply, in 1819, to such charges; "you have not seen the nice, clean, neat houses of the farmers of Long Island, in New England, in the Quaker counties of Pennsylvania; you have seen nothing but the smoke-dried ultramontanians." Yet Cobbett drew a sharp contrast between the laborer's neat cottage familiar to him in Surrey and Hampshire, and the "shell of boards" which the American occupied, "all around him as barren as a sea-beach." He added, too, that "the example of neatness was wanting;" no one taught it by showing its charm. Felix de Beaujour, otherwise not an enthusiastic American, paid a warm compliment to the country in this single respect, although he seemed to have the cities chiefly in mind:—

> "American neatness must possess some very attractive quality, since it seduces every traveller; and there is no one of them who, in returning to his own country, does not wish to meet again there that air of ease and neatness which rejoiced his sight during his stay in the United States."

Almost every traveller discussed the question whether the Americans were a temperate people, or whether they drank more than the English. Temperate they certainly were not, when judged by a modern standard. Every one acknowledged that in the South and West drinking was occasionally excessive; but even in Pennsylvania and New England the universal taste for drams proved habits by no means strict. Every grown man took his noon toddy as a matter of course; and although few were seen publicly drunk, many were habitually affected by liquor. The earliest temperance movement, ten or twelve years later, was said to have had its source in the scandal caused by the occasional intoxication of ministers at their regular meetings. Cobbett thought drinking the national disease; at all hours of the day, he said, young men, "even little boys, at or under twelve years of age, go into stores and tip off their drams." The mere comparison with England proved that the evil was great, for the English and Scotch were among the largest consumers of beer and alcohol on the globe.

In other respects besides sobriety American manners and morals were subjects of much dispute, and if judged by the diatribes of travellers like Thomas Moore and H. W. Bülow, were below the level of Europe. Of all classes of statistics, moral statistics were least apt to be preserved. Even in England, social vices could be gauged only by the records of criminal and divorce courts; in America, police was wanting and a divorce suit almost, if not quite, unknown. Apart from some coarseness, society must have been pure; and the coarseness was mostly an English inheritance. Among New Englanders, Chief-Justice Parsons was the model of judicial, social, and religious propriety; yet Parsons, in 1808, presented to a lady a copy of "Tom Jones," with a letter calling attention to the adventures of Molly Seagrim and the usefulness of describing vice. Among the social sketches in the "Portfolio" were many allusions to the coarseness of Philadelphia society, and the manners common to tea-parties. "I heard from married ladies," said a writer in February, 1803, "whose station as mothers demanded from them a guarded conduct,—from young ladies, whose age forbids the audience of such conversation, and who using it modesty must disclaim,—indecent allusions, indelicate expressions, and even at times immoral innuendoes. A loud laugh or a coarse exclamation followed each of these, and the young ladies generally went through the form of raising their fans to their faces."

Yet public and private records might be searched long, before they revealed evidence of misconduct such as filled the press and formed one of the commonest topics of conversation in the society of England and France. Almost every American family, however respectable, could show some victim to intemperance among its men, but few were mortified by a public scandal due to its women.

If the absence of positive evidence did not prove American society to be as pure as its simple and primitive condition implied, the same conclusion would be reached by observing the earnestness with which critics collected every charge that could be brought against it, and by noting the substance of the whole. Tried by this test, the society of 1800 was often coarse and sometimes brutal, but, except for intemperance, was moral. Indeed, its chief offence, in the eyes of Europeans, was dulness. The amusements of a people were commonly a fair sign of social development, and the Americans were only beginning to amuse themselves. The cities were small and few in number, and the diversions were such as cost little and required but elementary knowledge. In New England, although the theatre had gained a firm foothold in Boston, Puritan feelings still forbade the running of horses.

"The principal amusements of the inhabitants," said Dwight, "are visiting, dancing, music, conversation, walking, riding, sailing, shooting at a mark, draughts, chess, and unhappily, in some of the larger towns, cards and dramatic exhibitions. A considerable amusement is also furnished in many places by the examination and exhibitions of the superior schools; and a more considerable one by the public exhibitions of colleges. Our countrymen also fish and hunt. Journeys taken for pleasure are very numerous, and are a very favorite object. Boys and young men play at foot-ball, cricket, quoits, and at many other sports of an athletic cast, and in the winter are peculiarly fond of skating. Riding in a sleigh, or sledge, is also a favorite diversion in New England."

President Dwight was sincere in his belief that college commencements and sleigh-riding satisfied the wants of his people; he looked upon whist as an unhappy dissipation, and upon the theatre as immoral. He had no occasion to condemn horse-racing, for no race-course was to be found in New England. The horse and the dog existed only in varieties little suited for sport. In colonial days New England produced one breed of horses worth preserving and developing,—the Narragansett pacer; but, to the regret even of the clergy, this animal almost disappeared, and in 1800 New England could show nothing to take its place. The germ of the trotter and the trotting-match, the first general popular amusement, could be seen in almost any country village, where the owners of horses were in the habit of trotting what were called scratch-races, for a quarter or half a mile from the door of the tavern, along the public road. Perhaps this amusement had already a right to be called a New-England habit, showing defined tastes; but the force of the popular instinct was not fully felt in Massachusetts, or even in New York, although there it was given full play. New York possessed a race-course, and made in 1792 a great stride toward popularity by importing the famous stallion "Messenger" to become the source of endless interest for future generations; but Virginia was the region where the American showed his true character as a lover of sport. Long before the Revolution the race-course was commonly established in Virginia and Maryland; English running-horses of pure blood—descendants of the Darley Arabian and the Godolphin Arabian—were imported, and racing became the chief popular entertainment. The long Revolutionary War, and the general ruin it caused, checked the habit and deteriorated the breed; but with returning prosperity Virginia showed that the instinct was stronger than ever. In 1798 "Diomed," famous as the sire of racers, was imported into the State, and future rivalry between Virginia and New York could be foreseen. In 1800 the Virginia race-course still remained at the head of American popular amusements.

In an age when the Prince of Wales and crowds of English gentlemen attended every prize-fight, and patronized Tom Crib, Dutch Sam, the Jew Mendoza, and the negro Molyneux, an Englishman could hardly have expected that a Virginia race-course should be free from vice; and perhaps travellers showed best the general morality of the people by their practice of dwelling on Virginia vices. They charged the Virginians with fondness for horse-racing, cock-fighting, betting, and drinking; but the popular habit which most shocked them, and with which books of travel filled pages of description, was the so-called rough-and-tumble fight. The practice was not one on which authors seemed likely to dwell; yet foreigners like Weld, and Americans like Judge Longstreet in "Georgia Scenes," united to give it a sort of grotesque dignity like that of a bull-fight, and under their treatment it became interesting as a popular habit. The rough-and-tumble fight differed from the ordinary prize-fight, or boxing-match, by the absence of rules. Neither kicking, tearing, biting, nor gouging was forbidden by the law of the ring. Brutal as the practice was, it was neither new nor exclusively Virginian. The English travellers who described it as American barbarism, might have seen the same sight in Yorkshire at the same date. The rough-and-tumble fight was English in origin, and was brought to Virginia and the Carolinas in early days, whence it spread to the Ohio and Mississippi. The habit attracted general notice because of its brutality in a society that showed few brutal instincts. Friendly foreigners like Liancourt were honestly shocked by it; others showed somewhat too plainly their pleasure at finding a vicious habit which they could consider a natural product of democratic society. Perhaps the description written by Thomas Ashe showed best not only the ferocity of the fight but also the antipathies of the writer, for Ashe had something of the artist in his touch, and he felt no love for Americans. The scene was at Wheeling. A Kentuckian and a Virginian were the combatants.

"Bulk and bone were in favor of the Kentuckian; science and craft in that of the Virginian. The former promised himself victory from his power; the latter from his science. Very few rounds had taken place or fatal blows given, before the Virginian contracted his whole form, drew up his arms to his face, with his hands nearly closed in a concave by the fingers being bent to the full extension of the flexors, and summoning up all his energy for one act of desperation, pitched himself into the bosom of his opponent. Before the effects of this could be ascertained, the sky was rent by the shouts of the multitude; and I could learn that the Virginian had expressed as much beauty and skill in his retraction and bound, as if he had been bred in a menagerie and practised action and attitude among panthers and wolves. The shock received by the Kentuckian, and the want of breath, brought him instantly to the ground. The Virginian never lost his hold. Like those bats of the South who never quit the subject on which they fasten till they taste blood, he kept his knees in his enemy's body; fixing his claws in his hair and his thumbs on his eyes, gave them an instantaneous start from their sockets. The sufferer roared aloud, but uttered no complaint. The citizens again shouted with joy."

Ashe asked his landlord whether this habit spread down the Ohio.

"I understood that it did, on the left-hand side, and that I would do well to land there as little as possible. . . . I again demanded how a stranger was to distinguish a good from a vicious house of entertainment. 'By previous inquiry, or, if that was impracticable, a tolerable judgment could be formed from observing in the landlord a possession or an absence of ears.'"

The temper of the writer was at least as remarkable in this description as the scene he pretended to describe, for Ashe's Travels were believed to have been chiefly imaginary; but no one denied the roughness of the lower classes in the South and Southwest, nor was roughness wholly confined to them. No prominent man in Western society bore himself with more courtesy and dignity than Andrew Jackson of Tennessee, who in 1800 was candidate for the post of major-general of State militia, and had previously served as Judge on the Supreme Bench of his State; yet the fights in which he had been engaged exceeded belief.

Border society was not refined, but among its vices, as its virtues, few were permanent, and little idea could be drawn of the character that would at last emerge. The Mississippi boatman and the squatter on Indian lands were perhaps the most distinctly American type then existing, as far removed from the Old World as though Europe were a dream. Their language and imagination showed contact with Indians. A traveller on the levee at Natchez, in 1808, overheard a quarrel in a flatboat near by:—

"I am a man; I am a horse; I am a team," cried one voice; "I can whip any man in all Kentucky, by God!" "I am an alligator," cried the other; "half man, half horse; can whip any man on the Mississippi, by God!" "I am a man," shouted the first; "have the best horse, best dog, best gun, and handsomest wife in all Kentucky, by God!" "I am a Mississippi snapping-turtle," rejoined the second; "have bear's claws, alligator's teeth, and the devil's tail; can whip *any* man, by God!"

And on this usual formula of defiance the two fire-eaters began their fight, biting, gouging, and tearing. Foreigners were deeply impressed by barbarism such as this, and orderly emigrants from New England and Pennsylvania avoided contact with Southern drinkers and fighters; but even then they knew that with a new generation such traits must disappear, and that little could be judged of popular character from the habits of frontiersmen. Perhaps such vices deserved more attention when found in the older communities, but even there they were rather survivals of English low-life than products of a new soil, and they were given too much consequence in the tales of foreign travellers.

This was not the only instance where foreigners were struck by what they considered popular traits, which natives rarely noticed. Idle curiosity was commonly represented as universal, especially in the Southern settler who knew no other form of conversation:—

"Frequently have I been stopped by one of them," said Weld, "and without further preface asked where I was from, if I was acquainted with any news, where bound to, and finally my name. 'Stop, Mister! why, I guess now you be coming from the new State?' 'No, sir.' 'Why, then, I guess as how you be coming from Kentuck?' 'No, sir.' 'Oh, why, then, pray now where might you be coming from?' 'From the low country.' 'Why, you must have heard all the news, then; pray now, Mister, what might the price of bacon be in those parts?' 'Upon my word, my friend, I can't inform you.' 'Ay, ay; I see, Mister, you be'ent one of us. Pray now, Mister, what might your name be?'"

Almost every writer spoke with annoyance of the inquisitorial habits of New England and the impertinence of American curiosity. Complaints so common could hardly have lacked foundation, yet the Americans as a people were never loquacious, but inclined to be somewhat reserved, and they could not recognize the accuracy of the description. President Dwight repeatedly expressed astonishment at the charge, and asserted that in his large experience it had no foundation. Forty years later, Charles Dickens found complaint with Americans for taciturnity. Equally strange to modern experience were the continual complaints in books of travel that loungers and loafers, idlers of every description, infested the taverns, and annoyed respectable travellers both native and foreign. Idling seemed to be considered a popular vice, and was commonly associated with tippling. So completely did the practice disappear in the course of another generation that it could scarcely be recalled as offensive; but in truth less work was done by the average man in 1800 than in aftertimes, for there was actually less work to do. "Good country this for lazy fellows," wrote Wilson from Kentucky; "they plant corn, turn their pigs into the woods, and in the autumn feed upon corn and pork. They lounge about the rest of the year." The roar of the steam-engine had never been heard in the land, and the carrier's wagon was three weeks between Philadelphia and Pittsburg. What need for haste when days counted for so little? Why not lounge about the tavern when life had no better amusement to offer? Why mind one's own business when one's business would take care of itself?

Yet however idle the American sometimes appeared, and however large the class of tavern loafers may have actually been, the true American was active and industrious. No immigrant came to America for ease or idleness. If an English farmer bought land near New York, Philadelphia, or Baltimore, and made the most of his small capital, he found that while he could earn more money than in Surrey or Devonshire, he worked harder and suffered greater discomforts. The climate was trying; fever was common; the crops ran new risks from strange insects, drought, and violent weather; the weeds were annoying; the flies and mosquitoes tormented him and his cattle; laborers were scarce and indifferent; the slow and magisterial ways of England, where everything was made easy, must be exchanged for quick and energetic action; the farmer's own eye must see to every detail, his own hand must hold the plough and the scythe. Life was more exacting, and every such man in America was required to do, and actually did, the work of two such men in Europe. Few English farmers of the conventional class took kindly to American ways, or succeeded in adapting themselves to the changed conditions. Germans were more successful and became rich; but the poorer and more adventurous class, who had no capital, and cared nothing for the comforts of civilization, went West, to find a harder lot. When, after toiling for weeks, they reached the neighborhood of Genessee or the banks of some stream in southern Ohio or Indiana, they put up a rough cabin of logs with an earthen floor, cleared an acre or two of land, and planted Indian corn between the tree-stumps,—lucky if, like the Kentuckian, they had a pig to turn into the woods. Between April and October, Albert Gallatin used to say, Indian corn made the penniless immigrant a capitalist. New settlers suffered many of the ills that would have afflicted an army marching and fighting in a country of dense forest and swamp, with one sore misery besides,—that whatever trials the men endured, the burden bore most heavily upon the women and children. The chance of being shot or scalped by Indians was hardly worth considering when compared with the certainty of malarial fever, or the strange disease called milk-sickness, or the still more depressing homesickness, or the misery of nervous prostration, which wore out generation after generation of women and children on the frontiers, and left a tragedy in every log-cabin. Not for love of ease did men plunge into the wilderness. Few laborers of the Old World endured a harder lot, coarser fare, or anxieties and responsibilities greater than those of the Western emigrant. Not merely because he enjoyed the luxury of salt pork, whiskey, or even coffee three times a day did the American laborer claim superiority over the European.

A standard far higher than the average was common to the cities; but the city population was so small as to be trifling. Boston, New York, Philadelphia, and Baltimore together contained one hundred and eighty thousand inhabitants; and these were the only towns containing a white population of more than ten thousand persons. In a total population of more than five millions, this number of city people, as Jefferson and his friends rightly thought, was hardly American, for the true American was supposed to be essentially rural. Their comparative luxury was outweighed by the squalor of nine hundred thousand slaves alone.

From these slight notices of national habits no other safe inference could be drawn than that the people were still simple. The path their development might take was one of the many problems with which their future was perplexed. Such few habits as might prove to be fixed, offered little clew to the habits that might be adopted in the process of growth, and speculation was useless where change alone could be considered certain.

If any prediction could be risked, an observer might have been warranted in suspecting that the popular character was likely to be conservative, for as yet this trait was most marked, at least in the older societies of New England, Pennsylvania, and Virginia. Great as were the material obstacles in the path of the United States, the greatest obstacle of all was in the human mind. Down to the close of the eighteenth century no change had occurred in the world which warranted practical men in assuming that great changes were to come. Afterward, as time passed, and as science developed man's capacity to control Nature's forces, old-fashioned conservatism vanished from society, reappearing occasionally, like the stripes on a mule, only to prove its former existence; but during the eighteenth century the progress of America, except in political paths, had been less rapid than ardent reformers wished, and the reaction which followed the French Revolution made it seem even slower than it was. In 1723 Benjamin Franklin landed at Philadelphia, and with his loaf of bread under his arm walked along Market Street toward an immortality such as no American had then conceived. He died in 1790, after witnessing great political revolutions; but the intellectual revolution was hardly as rapid as he must, in his youth, have hoped.

In 1732 Franklin induced some fifty persons to found a subscription library, and his example and energy set a fashion which was generally followed. In 1800 the library he founded was still in existence; numerous small subscription libraries on the same model, containing fifty or a hundred volumes, were scattered in country towns; but all the public libraries in the United States—collegiate, scientific, or popular, endowed or unendowed—could hardly show fifty thousand volumes, including duplicates, fully one third being still theological.

Half a century had passed since Franklin's active mind drew the lightning from heaven, and decided the nature of electricity. No one in America had yet carried further his experiments in the field which he had made American. This inactivity was commonly explained as a result of the long Revolutionary War; yet the war had not prevented population and wealth from increasing, until Philadelphia in 1800 was far in advance of the Philadelphia which had seen Franklin's kite flying among the clouds.

In the year 1753 Franklin organized the postal system of the American colonies, making it self-supporting. No record was preserved of the number of letters then carried in proportion to the population, but in 1800 the gross receipts for postage were $320,000, toward which Pennsylvania contributed most largely,—the sum of $55,000. From letters the Government received in gross $290,000. The lowest rate of letter-postage was then eight cents. The smallest charge for letters carried more than a hundred miles was twelve and a half cents. If on an average ten letters were carried for a dollar, the whole number of letters was 2,900,000,—about one a year for every grown inhabitant.

Such a rate of progress could not be called rapid even by conservatives, and more than one stanch conservative thought it unreasonably slow. Even in New York, where foreign influence was active and the rewards of scientific skill were comparatively liberal, science hardly kept pace with wealth and population.

Noah Webster, who before beginning his famous dictionary edited the "New York Commercial Advertiser," and wrote on all subjects with characteristic confidence, complained of the ignorance of his countrymen. He claimed for the New Englanders an acquaintance with theology, law, politics, and light English literature; "but as to classical learning, history (civil and ecclesiastical), mathematics, astronomy, chemistry, botany, and natural history, excepting here and there a rare instance of a man who is eminent in some one of these branches, we may be said to have no learning at all, or a mere smattering." Although defending his countrymen from the criticisms of Dr. Priestley, he admitted that "our learning is superficial in a shameful degree,... our colleges are disgracefully destitute of books and philosophical apparatus,... and I am ashamed to own that scarcely a branch of science can be fully investigated in America for want of books, especially original works. This defect of our libraries I have experienced myself in searching for materials for the History of Epidemic Diseases.... As to libraries, we have no such things. There are not more than three or four tolerable libraries in America, and these are extremely imperfect. Great numbers of the most valuable authors have not found their way across the Atlantic."

This complaint was made in the year 1800, and was the more significant because it showed that Webster, a man equally at home in Philadelphia, New York, and Boston, thought his country's deficiencies greater than could be excused or explained by its circumstances. George Ticknor felt at least equal difficulty in explaining the reason why, as late as 1814, even good schoolbooks were rare in Boston, and a copy of Euripides in the original could not be bought at any book-seller's shop in New England. For some reason, the American mind, except in politics, seemed to these students of literature in a condition of unnatural sluggishness; and such complaints were not confined to literature or science. If Americans agreed in any opinion, they were united in wishing for roads; but even on that point whole communities showed an indifference, or hostility, that annoyed their contemporaries. President Dwight was a somewhat extreme conservative in politics and religion, while the State of Rhode Island was radical in both respects; but Dwight complained with bitterness unusual in his mouth that Rhode Island showed no spirit of progress. The subject of his criticism was an unfinished turnpike-road across the State.

"The people of Providence expended upon this road, as we are informed, the whole sum permitted by the Legislature. This was sufficient to make only those parts which I have mentioned. The turnpike company then applied to the Legislature for leave to expend such an additional sum as would complete the work. The Legislature refused. The principal reason for the refusal, as alleged by one of the members, it is said, was the following: that turnpikes and the establishment of religious worship had their origin in Great Britain, the government of which was a monarchy and the inhabitants slaves; that the people of Massachusetts and Connecticut were obliged by law to support ministers and pay the fare of turnpikes, and were therefore slaves also; that if they chose to be slaves they undoubtedly had a right to their choice, but that free-born Rhode Islanders ought never to submit to be priest-ridden, nor to pay for the privilege of travelling on the highway. This demonstrative reasoning prevailed, and the road continued in the state which I have mentioned until the year 1805. It was then completed, and free-born Rhode Islanders bowed their necks to the slavery of travelling on a good road."

President Dwight seldom indulged in sarcasm or exaggeration such as he showed in this instance; but he repeated only matters of notoriety in charging some of the most democratic communities with unwillingness to pay for good roads. If roads were to exist, they must be the result of public or private enterprise; and if the public in certain States would neither construct roads nor permit corporations to construct them, the entire Union must suffer for want of communication. So strong was the popular prejudice against paying for the privilege of travelling on a highway that in certain States, like Rhode Island and Georgia, turnpikes were long unknown, while in Virginia and North Carolina the roads were little better than where the prejudice was universal.

In this instance the economy of a simple and somewhat rude society accounted in part for indifference; in other cases, popular prejudice took a form less easily understood. So general was the hostility to Banks as to offer a serious obstacle to enterprise. The popularity of President Washington and the usefulness of his administration were impaired by his support of a national bank and a funding system. Jefferson's hostility to all the machinery of capital was shared by a great majority of the Southern people and a large minority in the North. For seven years the New York legislature refused to charter the first banking company in the State; and when in 1791 the charter was obtained, and the Bank fell into Federalist hands, Aaron Burr succeeded in obtaining banking privileges for the Manhattan Company only by concealing them under the pretence of furnishing a supply of fresh water to the city of New York.

This conservative habit of mind was more harmful in America than in other communities, because Americans needed more than older societies the activity which could alone partly compensate for the relative feebleness of their means compared with the magnitude of their task. Some instances of sluggishness, common to Europe and America, were hardly credible.

For more than ten years in England the steam-engines of Watt had been working, in common and successful use, causing a revolution in industry that threatened to drain the world for England's advantage; yet Europe during a generation left England undisturbed to enjoy the monopoly of steam. France and Germany were England's rivals in commerce and manufactures, and required steam for self-defence; while the United States were commercial allies of England, and needed steam neither for mines nor manufactures, but their need was still extreme. Every American knew that if steam could be successfully applied to navigation, it must produce an immediate increase of wealth, besides an ultimate settlement of the most serious material and political difficulties of the Union. Had both the national and State Governments devoted millions of money to this object, and had the citizens wasted, if necessary, every dollar in their slowly filling pockets to attain it, they would have done no more than the occasion warranted, even had they failed; but failure was not to be feared, for they had with their own eyes seen the experiment tried, and they did not dispute its success. For America this question had been settled as early as 1789, when John Fitch—a mechanic, without education or wealth, but with the energy of genius—invented engine and paddles of his own, with so much success that during a whole summer Philadelphians watched his ferry-boat plying daily against the river current. No one denied that his boat was rapidly, steadily, and regularly moved against wind and tide, with as much certainty and convenience as could be expected in a first experiment; yet Fitch's company failed. He could raise no more money; the public refused to use his boat or to help him build a better; they did not want it, would not believe in it, and broke his heart by their contempt. Fitch struggled against failure, and invented another boat moved by a screw. The Eastern public still proving indifferent, he wandered to Kentucky, to try his fortune on the Western waters. Disappointed there, as in

Philadelphia and New York, he made a deliberate attempt to end his life by drink; but the process proving too slow, he saved twelve opium pills from the physician's prescription, and was found one morning dead.

Fitch's death took place in an obscure Kentucky inn, three years before Jefferson, the philosopher president, entered the White House. Had Fitch been the only inventor thus neglected, his peculiarities and the defects of his steamboat might account for his failure; but he did not stand alone. At the same moment Philadelphia contained another inventor, Oliver Evans, a man so ingenious as to be often called the American Watt. He, too, invented a locomotive steam-engine which he longed to bring into common use. The great services actually rendered by this extraordinary man were not a tithe of those he would gladly have performed, had he found support and encouragement; but his success was not even so great as that of Fitch, and he stood aside while Livingston and Fulton, by their greater resources and influence, forced the steamboat on a sceptical public.

While the inventors were thus ready, and while State legislatures were offering mischievous monopolies for this invention, which required only some few thousand dollars of ready money, the Philosophical Society of Rotterdam wrote to the American Philosophical Society at Philadelphia, requesting to know what improvements had been made in the United States in the construction of steam-engines. The subject was referred to Benjamin H. Latrobe, the most eminent engineer in America, and his Report, presented to the Society in May, 1803, published in the Transactions, and transmitted abroad, showed the reasoning on which conservatism rested.

"During the general lassitude of mechanical exertion which succeeded the American Revolution," said Latrobe, "the utility of steam-engines appears to have been forgotten; but the subject afterward started into very general notice in a form in which it could not possibly be attended with much success. A sort of mania began to prevail, which indeed has not yet entirely subsided, for impelling boats by steam-engines. . . . For a short time a passage-boat, rowed by a steam-engine, was established between Borden-town and Philadelphia, but it was soon laid aside. . . . There are indeed general objections to the use of the steam-engine for impelling boats, from which no particular mode of application can be free. These are, first, the weight of the engine and of the fuel; second, the large space it occupies; third, the tendency of its action to rack the vessel and render it leaky; fourth, the expense of maintenance; fifth, the irregularity of its motion and the motion of the water in the boiler and cistern, and of the fuel-vessel in rough water; sixth, the difficulty arising from the liability of the paddles or oars to break if light, and from the weight, if made strong. Nor have I ever heard of an instance, verified by other testimony than that of the inventor, of a speedy and agreeable voyage having been performed in a steamboat of any construction. I am well aware that there are still many very respectable and ingenious men who consider the application of the steam-engine to the purpose of navigation as highly important and as very practicable, especially on the rapid waters of the Mississippi, and who would feel themselves almost offended at the expression of an opposite opinion. And perhaps some of the objections against it may be obviated. That founded on the expense and weight of the fuel may not for some years exist in the Mississippi, where there is a redundance of wood on the banks; but the cutting and loading will be almost as great an evil."

Within four years the steamboat was running, and Latrobe was its warmest friend. The dispute was a contest of temperaments, a divergence between minds, rather than a question of science; and a few visionaries such as those to whom Latrobe alluded—men like Chancellor Livingston, Joel Barlow, John Stevens, Samuel L. Mitchill, and Robert Fulton—dragged society forward. What but scepticism could be expected among a people thus asked to adopt the steamboat, when as yet the ordinary atmospheric steam-engine, such as had been in use in Europe for a hundred years, was practically unknown to them, and the engines of Watt were a fable? Latrobe's Report further said that in the spring of 1803, when he wrote, five steam-engines were at work in the United States,—one lately set up by the Manhattan Water Company in New York to supply the city with water; another in New York for sawing timber; two in Philadelphia, belonging to the city, for supplying water and running a rolling and slitting mill; and one at Boston employed in some manufacture. All but one of these were probably constructed after 1800, and Latrobe neglected to say whether they belonged to the old Newcomen type, or to Watt's manufacture, or to American invention; but he added that the chief American improvement on the steam-engine had been the construction of a wooden boiler, which developed sufficient power to work the Philadelphia pump at the rate of twelve strokes, of six feet, per minute. Twelve strokes a minute, or one stroke every five seconds, though not a surprising power, might have answered its purpose, had not the wooden boiler, as Latrobe admitted, quickly decomposed, and steam-leaks appeared at every bolt-hole.

If so eminent and so intelligent a man as Latrobe, who had but recently emigrated in the prime of life from England, knew little about Watt, and nothing about Oliver Evans, whose experience would have been well worth communicating to any philosophical society in Europe, the more ignorant and unscientific public could not feel faith in a force of which they knew nothing at all. For nearly two centuries the Americans had struggled on foot or horseback over roads not much better than trails, or had floated down rushing streams in open boats momentarily in danger of sinking or upsetting. They had at length, in the Eastern and Middle States, reached the point of constructing turnpikes and canals. Into these undertakings they put sums of money relatively large, for the investment seemed safe and the profits certain. Steam as a locomotive power was still a visionary idea, beyond their experience, contrary to European precedent, and exposed to a thousand risks. They regarded it as a delusion.

About three years after Latrobe wrote his Report on the steam-engine, Robert Fulton began to build the boat which settled forever the value of steam as a locomotive power. According to Fulton's well-known account of his own experience, he suffered almost as keenly as Fitch, twenty years before, under the want of popular sympathy:—

"When I was building my first steamboat at New York," he said, according to Judge Story's report, "the project was viewed by the public either with indifference or with contempt as a visionary scheme. My friends indeed were civil, but they were shy. They listened with patience to my explanations, but with a settled cast of incredulity upon their countenances. I felt the full force of the lamentation of the poet,—

'Truths would you teach, or save a sinking land,
All fear, none aid you, and few understand.'

As I had occasion to pass daily to and from the building-yard while my boat was in progress, I have often loitered unknown near the idle groups of strangers gathering in little circles, and heard various inquiries as to the object of this new vehicle. The language was uniformly that of scorn, or sneer, or ridicule. The loud laugh often rose at my expense; the dry jest; the wise calculation of losses and expenditures; the dull but endless repetition of the Fulton Folly. Never did a single encouraging remark, a bright hope, or a warm wish cross my path."

Possibly Fulton and Fitch, like other inventors, may have exaggerated the public apathy and contempt; but whatever was the precise force of the innovating spirit, conservatism possessed the world by right. Experience forced on men's minds the conviction that what had ever been must ever be. At the close of the eighteenth century nothing had occurred which warranted the belief that even the material difficulties of America could be removed. Radicals as extreme as Thomas Jefferson and Albert Gallatin were contented with avowing no higher aim than that America should reproduce the simpler forms of European republican society without European vices; and even this their opponents thought visionary. The United States had thus far made a single great step in advance of the Old World,—they had agreed to try the experiment of embracing half a continent in one republican system; but so little were they disposed to feel confidence in their success, that Jefferson himself did not look on this American idea as vital; he would not stake the future on so new an invention. "Whether we remain in one confederacy," he wrote in 1804, "or form into Atlantic and Mississippi confederations, I believe not very important to the happiness of either part." Even over his liberal mind history cast a spell so strong, that he thought the solitary American experiment of political confederation "not very important" beyond the Alleghanies.

The task of overcoming popular inertia in a democratic society was new, and seemed to offer peculiar difficulties. Without a scientific class to lead the way, and without a wealthy class to provide the means of experiment, the people of the United States were still required, by the nature of their problems, to become a speculating and scientific nation. They could do little without changing their old habit of mind, and without learning to love novelty for novelty's sake. Hitherto their timidity in using money had been proportioned to the scantiness of their means. Henceforward they were under every inducement to risk great stakes and frequent losses in order to win occasionally a thousand fold. In the colonial state they had naturally accepted old processes as the best, and European experience as final authority. As an independent people, with half a continent to civilize, they could not afford to waste time in following European examples, but must devise new processes of their own. A world which assumed that what had been must be, could not be scientific; yet in order to make the Americans a successful people, they must be roused to feel the necessity of scientific training. Until they were satisfied that knowledge was money, they would not insist upon high education; until they saw with their own eyes stones turned into gold, and vapor into cattle and corn, they would not learn the meaning of science.

Intellect of New England

WHETHER the United States were to succeed or fail in their economical and political undertakings, the people must still develop some intellectual life of their own, and the character of this development was likely to interest mankind. New conditions and hopes could hardly fail to produce a literature and arts more or less original. Of all possible triumphs, none could equal that which might be won in the regions of thought if the intellectual influence of the United States should equal their social and economical importance. Young as the nation was, it had already produced an American literature bulky and varied enough to furnish some idea of its probable qualities in the future, and the intellectual condition of the literary class in the United States at the close of the eighteenth century could scarcely fail to suggest both the successes and the failures of the same class in the nineteenth.

In intellectual tastes, as in all else, the Union showed well-marked divisions between New England, New York, Pennsylvania, and the Southern States. New England was itself divided between two intellectual centres,—Boston and New Haven. The Massachusetts and Connecticut schools were as old as the colonial existence; and in 1800 both were still alive, if not flourishing.

Society in Massachusetts was sharply divided by politics. In 1800 one half the population, represented under property qualifications by only some twenty thousand voters, was Republican. The other half, which cast about twenty-five thousand votes, included nearly every one in the professional and mercantile classes, and represented the wealth, social position, and education of the Commonwealth; but its strength lay in the Congregational churches and in the cordial union between the clergy, the magistracy, the bench and bar, and respectable society throughout the State. This union created what was unknown beyond New England,—an organized social system, capable of acting at command either for offence or defence, and admirably adapted for the uses of the eighteenth century.

Had the authority of the dominant classes in Massachusetts depended merely on office, the task of overthrowing it would have been as simple as it was elsewhere; but the New England oligarchy struck its roots deep into the soil, and was supported by the convictions of the people. Unfortunately the system was not and could not be quickly adapted to the movement of the age. Its starting-point lay in the educational system, which was in principle excellent; but it was also antiquated. Little change had been made in it since colonial times. The common schools were what they had been from the first; the academies and colleges were no more changed than the schools. On an average of ten years, from 1790 to 1800, thirty-nine young men annually took degrees from Harvard College; while during the ten years, 1766–1776, that preceded the Revolutionary War, forty-three bachelors of arts had been annually sent into the world, and even in 1720–1730 the average number had been thirty-five. The only sign of change was that in 1720–1730 about one hundred and forty graduates had gone into the Church, while in 1790–1800 only about eighty chose this career. At the earlier period the president, a professor of theology, one of mathematics, and four tutors gave instruction to the under-graduates. In 1800 the president, the professor of theology, the professor of mathematics, and a professor of Hebrew, created in 1765, with the four tutors did the same work. The method of instruction had not changed in the interval, being suited to children four-teen years of age; the instruction itself was poor, and the disci-pline was indifferent. Harvard College had not in eighty years made as much progress as was afterward made in twenty. Life was quickening within it as within all mankind,—the spirit and vivacity of the coming age could not be wholly shut out; but none the less the college resembled a priesthood which had lost the secret of its mysteries, and patiently stood holding the flickering torch before cold altars, until God should vouchsafe a new dispensation of sunlight.

Nevertheless, a medical school with three professors had been founded in 1783, and every year gave degrees to an average class of two doctors of medicine. Science had already a firm hold on the college, and a large part of the conservative clergy were distressed by the liberal tendencies which the governing body betrayed. This was no new thing. The college always stood somewhat in advance of society, and never joined heartily in dislike for liberal movements; but unfortunately it had been made for an instrument, and had never enjoyed the free use of its powers. Clerical control could not be thrown off, for if the college was compelled to support the clergy, on the other hand the clergy did much to support the college; and without the moral and material aid of this clerical body, which contained several hundred of the most respected and respectable citizens, clad in every town with the authority of spiritual magistrates, the college would have found itself bankrupt in means and character. The graduates passed from the college to the pulpit, and from the pulpit attempted to hold the college, as well as their own congregations, facing toward the past. "Let us guard against the insidious encroachments of *innovation*," they preached,—"that evil and beguiling spirit which is now stalk-ing to and fro through the earth, seeking whom he may de-stroy." These words were spoken by Jedediah Morse, a graduate of Yale in 1783, pastor of the church at Charlestown, near

Boston, and still known in biographical dictionaries as "the father of American geography." They were contained in the Election Sermon of this worthy and useful man, delivered June 6, 1803; but the sentiment was not peculiar to him, or confined to the audience he was then addressing,—it was the burden of a thousand discourses enforced by a formidable authority.

The power of the Congregational clergy, which had lasted unbroken until the Revolution, was originally minute and inquisitory, equivalent to a police authority. During the last quarter of the century the clergy themselves were glad to lay aside the more odious watchfulness over their parishes, and to welcome social freedom within limits conventionally fixed; but their old authority had not wholly disappeared. In country parishes they were still autocratic. Did an individual defy their authority, the minister put his three-cornered hat on his head, took his silver-topped cane in his hand, and walked down the village street, knocking at one door and another of his best parishioners, to warn them that a spirit of license and of French infidelity was abroad, which could be repressed only by a strenuous and combined effort. Any man once placed under this ban fared badly if he afterward came before a bench of magistrates. The temporal arm vigorously supported the ecclesiastical will. Nothing tended so directly to make respectability conservative, and conservatism a fetich of respectability, as this union of bench and pulpit. The democrat had no caste; he was not respectable; he was a Jacobin,—and no such character was admitted into a Federalist house. Every dissolute intriguer, loose-liver, forger, false-coiner, and prison-bird; every hair-brained, loud-talking demagogue; every speculator, scoffer, and atheist,—was a follower of Jefferson; and Jefferson was himself the incarnation of their theories.

A literature belonging to this subject exists,—stacks of newspapers and sermons, mostly dull, and wanting literary merit. In a few of them Jefferson figured under the well-remembered disguises of Puritan politics: he was Ephraim, and had mixed himself among the people; had apostatized from his God and religion; gone to Assyria, and mingled himself among the heathen; "gray hairs are here and there upon him, yet he knoweth not;" or he was Jeroboam, who drave Israel from following the Lord, and made them sin a great sin. He had doubted the authority of revelation, and ventured to suggest that petrified shells found embedded in rocks fifteen thousand feet above sea-level could hardly have been left there by the Deluge, because if the whole atmosphere were condensed as water, its weight showed that the seas would be raised only fifty-two and a half feet. Sceptic as he was, he could not accept the scientific theory that the ocean-bed had been uplifted by natural forces; but although he had thus instantly deserted this battery raised against revelation, he had still expressed the opinion that a universal deluge was *equally* unsatisfactory as an explanation, and had avowed preference for a profession of ignorance rather than a belief in error. He had said, "It does me no injury for my neighbors to say there are twenty gods, or no god," and that all the many forms of religious faith in the Middle States were "good enough, and sufficient to preserve peace and order." He was notoriously a deist; he probably ridiculed the doctrine of total depravity; and he certainly would never have part or portion in the blessings of the New Covenant, or be saved because of grace.

No abler or more estimable clergyman lived than Joseph Buckminster, the minister of Portsmouth, in New Hampshire, and in his opinion Jefferson was bringing a judgment upon the people.

"I would not be understood to insinuate," said he in his sermon on Washington's death, "that contemners of religious duties, and even men void of religious principle, may not have an attachment to their country and a desire for its civil and political prosperity,—nay, that they may not even expose themselves to great dangers, and make great sacrifices to accomplish this object; but by their impiety... they take away the heavenly defence and security of a people, and render it necessary for him who ruleth among the nations in judgment to testify his displeasure against those who despise his laws and contemn his ordinances."

Yet the congregational clergy, though still greatly respected, had ceased to be leaders of thought. Theological literature no longer held the prominence it had enjoyed in the days of Edwards and Hopkins. The popular reaction against Calvinism, felt rather than avowed, stopped the development of doctrinal theology; and the clergy, always poor as a class, with no weapons but their intelligence and purity of character, commonly sought rather to avoid than to challenge hostility. Such literary activity as existed was not clerical but secular. Its field was the Boston p ress, and its recognized literary champion was Fisher Ames.

The subject of Ames's thought was exclusively political. At that moment every influence combined to maintain a stationary condition in Massachusetts politics. The manners and morals of the people were pure and simple; their society was democratic; in the worst excesses of their own revolution they had never become savage or bloodthirsty; their experience could not explain, nor could their imagination excuse, wild popular excesses; and when in 1793 the French nation seemed mad with the frenzy of its recovered liberties, New England looked upon the bloody and blasphemous work with such horror as religious citizens could not but feel. Thenceforward the mark of a wise and good man was that he abhorred the French Revolution, and believed democracy to be its cause. Like Edmund Burke, they listened to no argument: "It is a vile, illiberal school, this French Academy of the sans-culottes; there is nothing in it that is fit for a gentleman to learn." The answer to every democratic suggestion ran in a set phrase, "Look at France!" This idea became a monomania with the New England leaders, and took exclusive hold of Fisher Ames, their most brilliant writer and talker, until it degenerated into a morbid illusion. During the last few months of his life, even so late as 1808, this dying man could scarcely speak of his children without expressing his fears of their future servitude to the French. He believed his alarms to be shared by his friends. "Our days," he wrote, "are made heavy with the pressure of anxiety, and our nights restless with visions of horror. We listen to the clank of chains, and overhear the whispers of assassins. We mark the barbarous dissonance of mingled rage and triumph in the yell of an infuriated mob; we see the dismal glare of their burnings, and scent the loathsome steam of human victims offered in sacrifice." In theory the French Revolution was not an argument or a proof, but only an illustration, of the workings of divine law; and what had happened in France must sooner or later happen in America if the ignorant and vicious were to govern the wise and good.

The bitterness against democrats became intense after the month of May, 1800, when the approaching victory of Jefferson was seen to be inevitable. Then for the first time the clergy and nearly all the educated and respectable citizens of New England began to extend to the national government the hatred which they bore to democracy. The expressions of this mixed antipathy filled volumes. "Our country," wrote Fisher Ames in 1803, "is too big for union, too sordid for patriotism, too democratic for liberty. What is to become of it, he who made it best knows. Its vice will govern it, by practising upon its folly. This is ordained for democracies." He explained why this inevitable fate awaited it. "A democracy cannot last. Its nature ordains that its next change shall be into a military despotism,—of all known governments perhaps the most prone to shift its head, and the slowest to mend its vices. The reason is that the tyranny of what is called the people, and that by the sword, both operate alike to debase and corrupt, till there are neither men left with the spirit to desire liberty, nor morals with the power to sustain justice. Like the burning pestilence that destroys the human body, nothing can subsist by its dissolution but vermin." George Cabot, whose political opinions were law to the wise and good, held the same convictions. "Even in New England," wrote Cabot in 1804, "where there is among the body of the people more wisdom and virtue than in any other part of the United States, we are full of errors which no reasoning could eradicate, if there were a Lycurgus in every village. We are democratic altogether, and I hold democracy in its natural operation to be the government of the worst."

Had these expressions of opinion been kept to the privacy of correspondence, the public could have ignored them; but so strong were the wise and good in their popular following, that every newspaper seemed to exult in denouncing the people. They urged the use of force as the protection of wisdom and virtue. A paragraph from Dennie's "Portfolio," reprinted by all the Federalist newspapers in 1803, offered one example among a thousand of the infatuation which possessed the Federalist press, neither more extravagant nor more treasonable than the rest:—

"A democracy is scarcely tolerable at any period of national history. Its omens are always sinister, and its powers are unpropitious. It is on its trial here, and the issue will be civil war, desolation, and anarchy. No wise man but discerns its imperfections, no good man but shudders at its miseries, no honest man but proclaims its fraud, and no brave man but draws his sword against its force. The institution of a scheme of policy so radically contemptible and vicious is a memorable example of what

the villany of some men can devise, the folly of others receive, and both establish in spite of reason, reflection,
and sensation."

The Philadelphia grand jury indicted Dennie for this paragraph as a seditious libel, but it was not more expressive than
the single word uttered by Alexander Hamilton, who owed no
small part of his supremacy to the faculty of expressing the
prejudices of his followers more tersely than they themselves
could do. Compressing the idea into one syllable, Hamilton, at
a New York dinner, replied to some democratic sentiment by
striking his hand sharply on the table and saying, "Your people,
sir,—your people is a great *beast*!"

The political theories of these ultra-conservative New Englanders did not require the entire exclusion of all democratic
influence from government. "While I hold," said Cabot, "that a
government altogether popular is in effect a government of the
populace, I maintain that no government can be relied on that
has not a material portion of the democratic mixture in its
composition." Cabot explained what should be the true portion of democratic mixture: "If no man in New England could
vote for legislators who was not possessed in his own right of
two thousand dollars' value *in land*, we could do something
better." The Constitution of Massachusetts already restricted
the suffrage to persons "having a freehold estate within the
commonwealth of an annual income of three pounds, or any
estate of the value of sixty pounds." A further restriction to
freeholders whose estate was worth two thousand dollars would
hardly have left a material mixture of any influence which democrats would have recognized as theirs.

Meanwhile even Cabot and his friends Ames and Colonel
Hamilton recognized that the reform they wished could be effected only with the consent of the people; and firm in the conviction that democracy must soon produce a crisis, as in Greece

and Rome, in England and France, when political power must revert to the wise and good, or to the despotism of a military chief, they waited for the catastrophe they foresaw. History and their own experience supported them. They were right, so far as human knowledge could make them so; but the old spirit of Puritan obstinacy was more evident than reason or experience in the simple-minded, overpowering conviction with which the clergy and serious citizens of Massachusetts and Connecticut, assuming that the people of America were in the same social condition as the contemporaries of Catiline and the adherents of Robespierre, sat down to bide their time until the tempest of democracy should drive the frail government so near destruction that all men with one voice should call on God and the Federalist prophets for help. The obstinacy of the race was never better shown than when, with the sunlight of the nineteenth century bursting upon them, these resolute sons of granite and ice turned their faces from the sight, and smiled in their sardonic way at the folly or wickedness of men who could pretend to believe the world improved because henceforth the ignorant and vicious were to rule the United States and govern the churches and schools of New England.

Even Boston, the most cosmopolitan part of New England, showed no tendency in its educated classes to become American in thought or feeling. Many of the ablest Federalists, and among the rest George Cabot, Theophilus Parsons, and Fisher Ames, shared few of the narrower theological prejudices of their time, but were conservatives of the English type, whose alliance with the clergy betrayed as much policy as religion, and whose intellectual life was wholly English. Boston made no strong claim to intellectual prominence. Neither clergy, lawyers, physicians, nor literary men were much known beyond the State. Fisher Ames enjoyed a wider fame; but Ames's best political writing was saturated with the despair of the tomb to which his wasting body was condemned. Five years had passed since he closed his famous speech on the British Treaty with the foreboding that if the treaty were not carried into effect, "even I, slender and almost broken as my hold upon life is, may outlive the government and constitution of my country." Seven years more were to pass in constant dwelling upon the same theme, in accents more and more despondent, before the long-expected grave closed over him, and his warning voice ceased to echo painfully on the air. The number of his thorough-going admirers was small, if his own estimate was correct. "There are," he said, "not many, perhaps not five hundred, even among the Federalists, who yet allow themselves to view the progress of licentiousness as so speedy, so sure, and so fatal as the deplorable experience of our country shows that it is, and the evidence of history and the constitution of human nature demonstrate that it must be." These five hundred, few as they were, comprised most of the clergy and the State officials, and overawed large numbers more.

Ames was the mouthpiece in the press of a remarkable group, of which George Cabot was the recognized chief in wisdom, and Timothy Pickering the most active member in national politics. With Ames, Cabot, and Pickering, joined in confidential relations, was Theophilus Parsons, who in the year 1800 left Newburyport for Boston. Parsons was an abler man than either Cabot, Ames, or Pickering, and his influence was great in holding New England fast to an independent course which could end only in the overthrow of the Federal constitution which these men had first pressed upon an unwilling people; but though gifted with strong natural powers, backed by laborious study and enlivened by the ready and somewhat rough wit native to New England, Parsons was not bold on his own account; he was felt rather than seen, and although ever ready in private to advise strong measures, he commonly let others father them before the world.

These gentlemen formed the Essex Junto, so called from the

county of Essex where their activity was first felt. According to Ames, not more than five hundred men fully shared their opinions; but Massachusetts society was so organized as to make their influence great, and experience foretold that as the liberal Federalists should one by one wander to the Democratic camp where they belonged, the conservatism of those who remained would become more bitter and more absolute as the Essex Junto represented a larger and larger proportion of their numbers.

Nevertheless, the reign of old-fashioned conservatism was near its end. The New England Church was apparently sound; even Unitarians and Baptists were recognized as parts of one fraternity. Except a few Roman and Anglican bodies, all joined in the same worship, and said little on points of doctrinal difference. No one had yet dared to throw a firebrand into the temple; but Unitarians were strong among the educated and wealthy class, while the tendencies of a less doctrinal religious feeling were shaping themselves in Harvard College. William Ellery Channing took his degree in 1798, and in 1800 was a private tutor in Virginia. Joseph Stevens Buckminster, thought by his admirers a better leader than Channing, graduated in 1800, and was teaching boys to construe their Latin exercises at Exeter Academy. Only the shell of orthodoxy was left, but respectable society believed this shell to be necessary as an example of Christian unity and a safeguard against more serious innovations. No one could fail to see that the public had lately become restive under its antiquated discipline. The pulpits still fulminated against the fatal tolerance which within a few years had allowed theatres to be opened in Boston, and which scandalized God-fearing men by permitting public advertisements that "Hamlet" and "Othello" were to be performed in the town founded to protest against worldly pageants. Another innovation was more strenuously resisted. Only within the last thirty years had Sunday travel been allowed even in England; in Massachusetts and Connecticut it was still forbidden by law, and the law was enforced. Yet not only travellers, but inn-keepers and large numbers of citizens connived at Sunday travel, and it could not long be prevented. The clergy saw their police authority weakening year by year, and understood, without need of many words, the tacit warning of the city congregations that in this world they must be allowed to amuse themselves, even though they were to suffer for it in the next.

The longing for amusement and freedom was a reasonable and a modest want. Even the young theologians, the Buckminsters and Channings, were hungry for new food. Boston was little changed in appearance, habits, and style from what it had been under its old king. When young Dr. J. C. Warren returned from Europe about the year 1800, to begin practice in Boston, he found gentlemen still dressed in colored coats and figured waistcoats, short breeches buttoning at the knee, long boots with white tops, ruffled shirts and wristbands, a white cravat filled with what was called a "pudding," and for the elderly, cocked hats, and wigs which once every week were sent to the barber's to be dressed,—so that every Saturday night the barbers' boys were seen carrying home piles of wig-boxes in readiness for Sunday's church. At evening parties gentlemen appeared in white small-clothes, silk stockings and pumps, with a colored or white waistcoat. There were few hackney-coaches, and ladies walked to evening entertainments. The ancient minuet was danced as late as 1806. The waltz was not yet tolerated.

Fashionable society was not without charm. In summer Southern visitors appeared, and admired the town, with its fashionable houses perched on the hillsides, each in its own garden, and each looking seaward over harbor and islands. Boston was then what Newport afterward became, and its only rival as a summer watering-place in the North was Ballston, whither society was beginning to seek health before finding it a little farther away at Saratoga. Of intellectual amusement there was little more at one place than at the other, except that the

Bostonians devoted themselves more seriously to church-going and to literature. The social instinct took shape in varied forms, but was highly educated in none; while the typical entertainment in Boston, as in New York, Philadelphia, and Charleston, was the state dinner,—not the light, feminine triviality which France introduced into an amusement-loving world, but the serious dinner of Sir Robert Walpole and Lord North, where gout and plethora waited behind the chairs; an effort of animal endurance.

There was the arena of intellectual combat, if that could be called combat where disagreement in principle was not tolerated. The talk of Samuel Johnson and Edmund Burke was the standard of excellence to all American society that claimed intellectual rank, and each city possessed its own circle of Federalist talkers. Democrats rarely figured in these entertainments, at least in fashionable private houses. "There was no exclusiveness," said a lady who long outlived the time; "but I should as soon have expected to see a cow in a drawing-room as a Jacobin." In New York, indeed, Colonel Burr and the Livingstons may have held their own, and the active-minded Dr. Mitchill there, like Dr. Eustis in Boston, was an agreeable companion. Philadelphia was comparatively cosmopolitan; in Baltimore the Smiths were a social power; and Charleston, after deserting Federal principles in 1800, could hardly ignore Democrats; but Boston society was still pure. The clergy took a prominent part in conversation, but Fisher Ames was the favorite of every intelligent company; and when Gouverneur Morris, another brilliant talker, visited Boston, Ames was pitted against him.

The intellectual wants of the community grew with the growing prosperity; but the names of half-a-dozen persons could hardly be mentioned whose memories survived by intellectual work made public in Massachusetts between 1783 and 1800. Two or three local historians might be numbered, including Jeremy Belknap, the most justly distinguished. Jedediah

Morse the geographer was well known; but not a poet, a novelist, or a scholar could be named. Nathaniel Bowditch did not publish his "Practical Navigator" till 1800, and not till then did Dr. Waterhouse begin his struggle to introduce vaccination. With the exception of a few Revolutionary statesmen and elderly clergymen, a political essayist like Ames, and lawyers like Samuel Dexter and Theophilus Parsons, Massachusetts could show little that warranted a reputation for genius; and, in truth, the intellectual prominence of Boston began as the conservative system died out, starting with the younger Buckminster several years after the century opened.

The city was still poorer in science. Excepting the medical profession, which represented nearly all scientific activity, hardly a man in Boston got his living either by science or art. When in the year 1793 the directors of the new Middlesex Canal Corporation, wishing to bring the Merrimac River to Boston Harbor, required a survey of an easy route not thirty miles long, they could find no competent civil engineer in Boston, and sent to Philadelphia for an Englishman named Weston, engaged on the Delaware and Schuylkill Canal.

Possibly a few Bostonians could read and even speak French; but Germany was nearly as unknown as China, until Madame de Staël published her famous work in 1814. Even then young George Ticknor, incited by its account of German university education, could find neither a good teacher nor a dictionary, nor a German book in the shops or public libraries of the city or at the college in Cambridge. He had discovered a new world.

Pope, Addison, Akenside, Beattie, and Young were still the reigning poets. Burns was accepted by a few; and copies of a volume were advertised by book-sellers, written by a new poet called Wordsworth. America offered a fair demand for new books, and anything of a light nature published in England was sure to cross the ocean. Wordsworth crossed with the rest, and his "Lyrical Ballads" were reprinted in 1802, not in Boston or New York, but in Philadelphia, where they were read and praised. In default of other amusements, men read what no one could have endured had a choice of amusements been open. Neither music, painting, science, the lecture-room, nor even magazines offered resources that could rival what was looked upon as classical literature. Men had not the alternative of listening to political discussions, for stump-speaking was a Southern practice not yet introduced into New England, where such a political canvass would have terrified society with dreams of Jacobin license. The clergy and the bar took charge of politics; the tavern was the club and the forum of political discussion; but for those who sought other haunts, and especially for women, no intellectual amusement other than what was called "belles-lettres" existed to give a sense of occupation to an active mind. This keen and innovating people, hungry for the feast that was almost served, the Walter Scotts and Byrons so near at hand, tried meanwhile to nourish themselves with husks.

Afraid of Shakspeare and the drama, trained to the standards of Queen Anne's age, and ambitious beyond reason to excel, the New Englanders attempted to supply their own wants. Massachusetts took no lead in the struggle to create a light literature, if such poetry and fiction could be called light. In Connecticut the Muses were most obstinately wooed; and there, after the Revolutionary War, a persistent effort was made to give prose the form of poetry. The chief of the movement was Timothy Dwight, a man of extraordinary qualities, but one on whom almost every other mental gift had been conferred in fuller measure than poetical genius. Twenty-five years had passed since young Dwight, fresh from Yale College, began his career by composing an epic poem, in eleven books and near ten thousand lines, called "The Conquest of Canaan." In the fervor of patriotism, before independence was secured or the

French Revolution imagined, he pictured the great Hebrew leader Joshua preaching the Rights of Man, and prophesying the spread of his "sons" over America:—

> "Then o'er wide lands, as blissful Eden bright,
> Type of the skies, and seats of pure delight,
> Our sons with prosperous course shall stretch their sway,
> And claim an empire spread from sea to sea;
> In one great whole th' harmonious tribes combine,
> Trace Justice' path, and choose their chiefs divine;
> On Freedom's base erect the heavenly plan,
> Teach laws to reign, and save the Rights of Man.
> Then smiling Art shall wrap the fields in bloom,
> Fine the rich ore, and guide the useful loom;
> Then lofty towers in golden pomp arise,
> Then spiry cities meet auspicious skies;
> The soul on Wisdom's wing sublimely soar,
> New virtues cherish and new truths explore;
> Through Time's long tract our name celestial run,
> Climb in the east and circle with the sun;
> And smiling Glory stretch triumphant wings
> O'er hosts of heroes and o'er tribes of kings."

A world of eighteenth-century thought, peopled with personifications, lay buried in the ten thousand lines of President Dwight's youthful poem. Perhaps in the year 1800, after Jefferson's triumph, Dwight would have been less eager that his hero should save the Rights of Man; by that time the phrase had acquired a flavor of French infidelity which made it unpalatable to good taste. Yet the same Jeffersonian spirit ran through Dwight's famous national song, which was also written in the Revolutionary War:—

"Columbia, Columbia, to glory arise,
The queen of the world and child of the skies!

   .   .   .   .

Thy heroes the rights of mankind shall defend,
And triumph pursue them, and glory attend.

     .   .   .   .   .   .

While the ensigns of union in triumph unfurled
Hush the tumult of war and give peace to the world."

"Peace to the world" was the essence of Jeffersonian principles, worth singing in something better than jingling metre and indifferent rhyme; but President Dwight's friends in 1800 no longer sang this song. More and more conservative as he grew older, he published in 1797 an orthodox "Triumph of Infidelity," introduced by a dedication to Voltaire. His rebuke to mild theology was almost as severe as that to French deism:—

"There smiled the smooth divine, unused to wound
The sinner's heart with Hell's alarming sound."

His poetical career reached its climax in 1794 in a clerical Connecticut pastoral in seven books, called "Greenfield Hill." Perhaps his verses were not above the level of the Beatties and Youngs he imitated; but at least they earned for President Dwight no mean reputation in days when poetry was at its lowest ebb, and made him the father of a school.

One quality gave respectability to his writing apart from genius. He loved and believed in his country. Perhaps the uttermost depths of his nature were stirred only by affection for the Connecticut Valley; but after all where was human nature more respectable than in that peaceful region? What had the United States then to show in scenery and landscape more beautiful or more winning than that country of meadow and mountain?

Patriotism was no ardent feeling among the literary men of the time, whose general sentiment was rather expressed by Cliffton's lines:—

> "In these cold shades, beneath these shifting skies,
> Where Fancy sickens, and where Genius dies,
> Where few and feeble are the Muse's strains,
> And no fine frenzy riots in the veins,
> There still are found a few to whom belong
> The fire of virtue and the soul of song."

William Cliffton, a Pennsylvania Friend, who died in 1799 of consumption, in his twenty-seventh year, knew nothing of the cold shades and shifting skies which chilled the genius of European poets; he knew only that America cared little for such genius and fancy as he could offer, and he rebelled against the neglect. He was better treated than Wordsworth, Keats, or Shelley; but it was easy to blame the public for dulness and indifference, though readers were kinder than authors had a right to expect. Even Cliffton was less severe than some of his contemporaries. A writer in the "Boston Anthology," for January, 1807, uttered in still stronger words the prevailing feeling of the literary class:—

> "We know that in this land, where the spirit of democracy is everywhere diffused, we are exposed as it were to a poisonous atmosphere, which blasts everything beautiful in nature, and corrodes everything elegant in art; we know that with us 'the rose-leaves fall ungathered,' and we believe that there is little to praise and nothing to admire in most of the objects which would first present themselves to the view of a stranger."

Yet the American world was not unsympathetic toward Cliffton and his rivals, though they strained prose through their sieves of versification, and showed open contempt for their audience. Toward President Dwight the public was even generous; and he returned the generosity with parental love and condescension which shone through every line he wrote. For some years his patriotism was almost as enthusiastic as that of Joel Barlow. He was among the numerous rivals of Macaulay and Shelley for the honor of inventing the stranger to sit among the ruins of St. Paul's; and naturally America supplied the explorer who was to penetrate the forest of London and indulge his national self-complacency over ruined temples and towers.

> "Some unknown wild, some shore without a name,
> In all thy pomp shall then majestic shine
> As silver-headed Time's slow years decline.
> Not ruins only meet th' inquiring eye;
> Where round yon mouldering oak vain brambles twine,
> The filial stem, already towering high,
> Erelong shall stretch his arms and nod in yonder sky."

From these specimens of President Dwight's poetry any critic, familiar with the time, could infer that his prose was sensible and sound. One of the few books of travel which will always retain value for New Englanders was written by President Dwight to describe his vacation rambles; and although in his own day no one would have ventured to insult him by calling these instructive volumes amusing, the quaintness which here and there gave color to the sober narrative had a charm of its own. How could the contrast be better expressed between volatile Boston and orthodox New Haven than in Dwight's quiet reproof, mixed with paternal tenderness? The Bostonians, he said, were distinguished by a lively imagination, ardor, and sensibility; they were "more like the Greeks than the Romans;" admired where graver people would only approve; applauded or hissed where another audience would be silent; their language was frequently hyperbolical, their pictures highly colored; the tea shipped to Boston was destroyed,—in New York and Philadelphia it was stored; education in Boston was superficial, and Boston women showed the effects of this misfortune, for they practised accomplishments only that they might be admired, and were taught from the beginning to regard their dress as a momentous concern.

Under Dwight's rule the women of the Connecticut Valley were taught better; but its men set to the Bostonians an example of frivolity without a parallel, and they did so with the connivance of President Dwight and under the lead of his brother Theodore. The frivolity of the Hartford wits, as they were called, was not so light as that of Canning and the "Anti-Jacobin," but had it been heavier than the "Conquest of Canaan" itself, it would still have found no literary rivalry in Boston. At about the time when Dwight composed his serious epic, another tutor at Yale, John Trumbull, wrote a burlesque epic in Hudibrastic verse, "McFingal," which his friend Dwight declared to be not inferior to "Hudibras" in wit and humor, and in every other respect superior. When "Hudibras" was published, more than a hundred years before, Mr. Pepys remarked: "It hath not a good liking in me, though I had tried but twice or three times reading to bring myself to think it witty." After the lapse of more than another century, the humor of neither poem may seem worth imitation; but to Trumbull in 1784 Butler was a modern classic, for the standard of taste between 1663 and 1784 changed less than in any twenty years of the following century. "McFingal" was a success, and laid a solid foundation for the coming school of Hartford wits. Posterity ratified the verdict of

Trumbull's admirers by preserving for daily use a few of his lines quoted indiscriminately with Butler's best:—

"What has posterity done for us?"

"Optics sharp it needs, I ween,
To see what is not to be seen."

"A thief ne'er felt the halter draw
With good opinion of the law."

Ten years after the appearance of "McFingal," and on the strength of its success, Trumbull, Lemuel Hopkins, Richard Alsop, Theodore Dwight, Joel Barlow, and others began a series of publications, "The Anarchiad," "The Echo," "The Guillotine," and the like, in which they gave tongue to their wit and sarcasm. As Alsop described the scene,—

"Begrimed with blood where erst the savage fell,
Shrieked the wild war-whoop with infernal yell,
The Muses sing; lo, Trumbull wakes the lyre.

    .   .   .   .

Majestic Dwight, sublime in epic strain,
Paints the fierce horrors of the crimson plain;
And in Virgilian Barlow's tuneful lines
With added splendor great Columbus shines."

Perhaps the Muses would have done better by not interrupting the begrimed savage; for Dwight, Trumbull, Alsop, and Hopkins, whatever their faults, were Miltonic by the side of Joel Barlow. Yet Barlow was a figure too important in American history to be passed without respectful attention. He expressed better than any one else that side of Connecticut character which roused at the same instant the laughter and the respect of men. Every human influence twined about his career and lent it interest; every forward movement of his time had his sympathy, and few steps in progress were made which he did not assist. His ambition, above the lofty ambition of Jefferson, made him aspire to be a Connecticut Mæcenas and Virgil in one; to patronize Fulton and employ Smirke; counsel Jefferson and contend with Napoleon. In his own mind a figure such as the world rarely saw,—a compound of Milton, Rousseau, and the Duke of Bridgewater,—he had in him so large a share of conceit, that tragedy, which would have thrown a solemn shadow over another man's life, seemed to render his only more entertaining. As a poet, he undertook to do for his native land what Homer had done for Greece and Virgil for Rome, Milton for England and Camoens for Portugal,—to supply America with a great epic, without which no country could be respectable; and his "Vision of Columbus," magnified afterward into the "Columbiad," with a magnificence of typography and illustration new to the United States, remained a monument of his ambition. In this vision Columbus was shown a variety of coming celebrities, including all the heroes of the Revolutionary War:—

"Here stood stern Putnam, scored with ancient scars,
The living records of his country's wars;
Wayne, like a moving tower, assumes his post,
Fires the whole field, and is himself a host;
Undaunted Stirling, prompt to meet his foes,
And Gates and Sullivan for action rose;
Macdougal, Clinton, guardians of the State,
Stretch the nerved arm to pierce the depth of fate;
Moultrie and Sumter lead their banded powers;
Morgan in front of his bold riflers towers,
His host of keen-eyed marksmen, skilled to pour

Their slugs unerring from the twisted bore;
No sword, no bayonet they learn to wield,
They gall the flank, they skirt the battling field,
Cull out the distant foe in full horse speed,
Couch the long tube and eye the silver bead,
Turn as he turns, dismiss the whizzing lead,
And lodge the death-ball in his heedless head."

More than seven thousand lines like these furnished constant pleasure to the reader, the more because the "Columbiad" was accepted by the public in a spirit as serious as that in which it was composed. The Hartford wits, who were bitter Federalists, looked upon Barlow as an outcast from their fold, a Jacobin in politics, and little better than a French atheist in religion; but they could not deny that his poetic garments were of a piece with their own. Neither could they without great ingratitude repudiate his poetry as they did his politics, for they themselves figured with Manco Capac, Montezuma, Raleigh, and Pocahontas before the eyes of Columbus; and the world bore witness that Timothy Dwight, "Heaven in his eye and rapture on his tongue," tuned his "high harp" in Barlow's inspired verses. Europe was as little disposed as America to cavil; and the Abbé Grégoire assured Barlow in a printed letter that this monument of genius and typography would immortalize the author and silence the criticisms of Pauw and other writers on the want of talent in America.

That the "Columbiad" went far to justify those criticisms was true; but on the other hand it proved something almost equivalent to genius. Dwight, Trumbull, and Barlow, whatever might be their differences, united in offering proof of the boundless ambition which marked the American character. Their aspirations were immense, and sooner or later such restless craving was sure to find better expression. Meanwhile Connecticut was a province by itself, a part of New England rather than of the United States. The exuberant patriotism of the Revolution was chilled by the steady progress of democratic principles in the Southern and Middle States, until at the election of Jefferson in 1800 Connecticut stood almost alone with no intellectual companion except Massachusetts, while the breach between them and the Middle States seemed to widen day by day. That the separation was only superficial was true; but the connection itself was not yet deep. An extreme Federalist partisan like Noah Webster did not cease working for his American language and literature because of the triumph of Jeffersonian principles elsewhere; Barlow became more American when his friends gained power; the work of the colleges went on unbroken; but prejudices, habits, theories, and laws remained what they had been in the past, and in Connecticut the influence of nationality was less active than ten, twenty, or even thirty years before. Yale College was but a reproduction of Harvard with stricter orthodoxy, turning out every year about thirty graduates, of whom nearly one fourth went into the Church. For the last ten years the number tended rather to diminish than to increase.

Evidently an intellectual condition like that of New England could not long continue. The thoughts and methods of the eighteenth century held possession of men's minds only because the movement of society was delayed by political passions. Massachusetts, and especially Boston, already contained a younger generation eager to strike into new paths, while forcibly held in the old ones. The more decidedly the college graduates of 1800 disliked democracy and its habits of thought, the more certain they were to compensate for political narrowness by freedom in fields not political. The future direction of the New England intellect seemed already suggested by the impossibility of going further in the line of President Dwight and Fisher Ames. Met by a barren negation on that side, thought was driven to some new channel; and the United States were the more concerned in the result because, with the training and literary habits of New Englanders and the new models already established in Europe for their guidance, they were likely again to produce something that would command respect.

Intellect of the Middle States

BETWEEN New England and the Middle States was a gap like that between Scotland and England. The conceptions of life were different. In New England society was organized on a system,—a clergy in alliance with a magistracy; universities supporting each, and supported in turn,—a social hierarchy, in which respectability, education, property, and religion united to defeat and crush the unwise and vicious. In New York wisdom and virtue, as understood in New England, were but lightly esteemed. From an early moment no small number of those who by birth, education, and property were natural leaders of the wise and virtuous, showed themselves ready to throw in their lot with the multitude. Yet New York, much more than New England, was the home of natural leaders and family alliances. John Jay, the governor; the Schuylers, led by Philip Schuyler and his son-in-law Alexander Hamilton; the Livingstons, led by Robert R. Livingston the chancellor, with a promising younger brother Edward nearly twenty years his junior, and a brother-in-law John Armstrong, whose name and relationship will be prominent in this narrative, besides Samuel Osgood, Morgan Lewis, and Smith Thompson, other connections by marriage with the great Livingston stock; the Clintons, headed by Governor George Clinton, and supported by the energy of De Witt his nephew, thirty years of age, whose close friend Ambrose Spencer was reckoned as one of the family; finally, Aaron Burr, of pure Connecticut Calvinistic blood, whose

two active lieutenants, William P. Van Ness and John Swart-
wout, were socially well connected and well brought up,—all
these Jays, Schuylers, Livingstons, Clintons, Burrs, had they
lived in New England, would probably have united in the support of their class, or abandoned the country; but being citizens
of New York they quarrelled. On one side Governor Jay, General Schuyler, and Colonel Hamilton were true to their principles. Rufus King, the American minister in London, by birth a
New Englander, adhered to the same connection. On the other
hand, George Clinton, like Samuel Adams in Boston, was a
Republican by temperament, and his protest against the Constitution made him leader of the Northern Republicans long
before Jefferson was mentioned as his rival. The rest were all
backsliders from Federalism,—and especially the Livingston
faction, who, after carefully weighing arguments and interests,
with one accord joined the mob of free-thinking democrats,
the "great beast" of Alexander Hamilton. Aaron Burr, who
prided himself on the inherited patrician quality of his mind
and manners, coldly assuming that wisdom and virtue were
powerless in a democracy, followed Chancellor Livingston into
the society of Cheetham and Paine. Even the influx of New
Englanders into the State could not save the Federalists; and in
May, 1800, after a sharp struggle, New York finally enrolled itself on the side of Jefferson and George Clinton.

Fortunately for society, New York possessed no church to
overthrow, or traditional doctrines to root out, or centuries of
history to disavow. Literature of its own it had little; of intellectual unity, no trace. Washington Irving was a boy of seventeen
wandering along the banks of the river he was to make famous;
Fenimore Cooper was a boy of eleven playing in the primitive
woods of Otsego, or fitting himself at Albany for entrance to
Yale College; William Cullen Bryant was a child of six in the
little village of Cummington, in western Massachusetts.

Political change could as little affect the educational system as it could affect history, church, or literature. In 1795, at the suggestion of Governor Clinton, an attempt had been made by the New York legislature to create a common-school system, and a sum of fifty thousand dollars was for five years annually applied to that object; but in 1800 the appropriation was exhausted, and the thirteen hundred schools which had been opened were declining. Columbia College, with a formidable array of unfilled professorships, and with fifteen or twenty annual graduates, stood apart from public affairs, although one of its professors, Dr. Samuel L. Mitchill, gave scientific reputation to the whole State. Like the poet Barlow, Mitchill was a universal genius,—a chemist, botanist, naturalist, physicist, and politician, who, to use the words of a shrewd observer, supported the Republican party because Jefferson was its leader, and supported Jefferson because he was a philosopher. Another professor of Columbia College, Dr. David Hosack, was as active as Dr. Mitchill in education, although he contented himself with private life, and did not, like Mitchill, reach the dignity of congressman and senator.

Science and art were still less likely to be harmed by a democratic revolution. For scientific work accomplished before 1800 New York might claim to excel New England; but the result was still small. A little botany and mineralogy, a paper on the dispute over yellow fever or vaccination, was the utmost that medicine could show; yet all the science that existed was in the hands of the medical faculty. Botany, chemistry, mineralogy, midwifery, and surgery were so closely allied that the same professor might regard them all as within the range of his instruction; and Dr. Mitchill could have filled in succession, without much difficulty, every chair in Columbia College as well as in the Academy of Fine Arts about to be established. A surgeon was assumed to be an artist. The Capitol at Washington was designed, in rivalry with a French architect, by Dr. William Thornton, an English physician, who in the course of two weeks' study at the Philadelphia Library gained enough knowledge of architecture to draw incorrectly an exterior elevation. When Thornton was forced to look for some one to help him over his difficulties, Jefferson could find no competent native American, and sent for Latrobe. Jefferson considered himself a better architect than either of them, and had he been a professor of materia medica at Columbia College, the public would have accepted his claim as reasonable.

The intellectual and moral character of New York left much to be desired; but on the other hand, had society adhered stiffly to what New England thought strict morals, the difficulties in the path of national development would have been increased. Innovation was the most useful purpose which New York could serve in human interests, and never was a city better fitted for its work. Although the great tide of prosperity had hardly begun to flow, the political character of city and State was already well defined in 1800 by the election which made Aaron Burr vice-president of the United States, and brought De Witt Clinton into public life as Burr's rival. De Witt Clinton was hardly less responsible than Burr himself for lowering the standard of New York politics, and indirectly that of the nation; but he was foremost in creating the Erie Canal. Chancellor Livingston was frequently charged with selfishness as great as that of Burr and Clinton; but he built the first steamboat, and gave immortality to Fulton. Ambrose Spencer's politics were inconsistent enough to destroy the good name of any man in New England; but he became a chief-justice of ability and integrity. Edward Livingston was a defaulter under circumstances of culpable carelessness, as the Treasury thought; but Gallatin, who dismissed him from office, lived to see him become the author of a celebrated code of civil law, and of the still more celebrated Nullification Proclamation. John Armstrong's character was so little admired that his own party could with difficulty be induced to give him high office; yet the reader will judge how

Armstrong compared in efficiency of public service with the senators who distrusted him.

New York cared but little for the metaphysical subtleties of Massachusetts and Virginia, which convulsed the nation with spasms almost as violent as those that, fourteen centuries before, distracted the Eastern Empire in the effort to establish the double or single nature of Christ. New York was indifferent whether the nature of the United States was single or multiple, whether they were a nation or a league. Leaving this class of questions to other States which were deeply interested in them, New York remained constant to no political theory. There society, in spite of its aristocratic mixture, was democratic by instinct; and in abandoning its alliance with New England in order to join Virginia and elect Jefferson to the Presidency, it pledged itself to principles of no kind, least of all to Virginia doctrines. The Virginians aimed at maintaining a society so simple that purity should suffer no danger, and corruption gain no foothold; and never did America witness a stranger union than when Jefferson, the representative of ideal purity, allied himself with Aaron Burr, the Livingstons and Clintons, in the expectation of fixing the United States in a career of simplicity and virtue. George Clinton indeed, a States-rights Republican of the old school, understood and believed the Virginia doctrines; but as for Aaron Burr, Edward Livingston, De Witt Clinton, and Ambrose Spencer,—young men whose brains were filled with dreams of a different sort,—what had such energetic democrats to do with the plough, or what share had the austerity of Cato and the simplicity of Ancus Martius in their ideals? The political partnership between the New York Republicans and the Virginians was from the first that of a business firm; and no more curious speculation could have been suggested to the politicians of 1800 than the question whether New York would corrupt Virginia, or Virginia would check the prosperity of New York.

In deciding the issue of this struggle, as in every other issue that concerned the Union, the voice which spoke in most potent tones was that of Pennsylvania. This great State, considering its political importance, was treated with little respect by its neighbors; and yet had New England, New York, and Virginia been swept out of existence in 1800, democracy could have better spared them all than have lost Pennsylvania. The only true democratic community then existing in the eastern States, Pennsylvania was neither picturesque nor troublesome. The State contained no hierarchy like that of New England; no great families like those of New York; no oligarchy like the planters of Virginia and South Carolina. "In Pennsylvania," said Albert Gallatin, "not only we have neither Livingstons nor Rensselaers, but from the suburbs of Philadelphia to the banks of the Ohio I do not know a single family that has any extensive influence. An equal distribution of property has rendered every individual independent, and there is among us true and real equality." This was not all. The value of Pennsylvania to the Union lay not so much in the democratic spirit of society as in the rapidity with which it turned to national objects. Partly for this reason the State made an insignificant figure in politics. As the nation grew, less and less was said in Pennsylvania of interests distinct from those of the Union. Too thoroughly democratic to fear democracy, and too much nationalized to dread nationality, Pennsylvania became the ideal American State, easy, tolerant, and contented. If its soil bred little genius, it bred still less treason. With twenty different religious creeds, its practice could not be narrow, and a strong Quaker element made it humane. If the American Union succeeded, the good sense, liberality, and democratic spirit of Pennsylvania had a right to claim credit for the result; and Pennsylvanians could afford to leave power and patronage to their neighbors, so long as their own interests were to decide the path of administration.

The people showed little of that acuteness which prevailed to the eastward of the Hudson. Pennsylvania was never smart, yet rarely failed to gain her objects, and never committed serious follies. To politics the Pennsylvanians did not take kindly. Perhaps their democracy was so deep an instinct that they knew not what to do with political power when they gained it; as though political power were aristocratic in its nature, and democratic power a contradiction in terms. On this ground rested the reputation of Albert Gallatin, the only Pennsylvanian who made a mark on the surface of national politics. Gallatin's celebrated financial policy carried into practice the doctrine that the powers of government, being necessarily irresponsible, and therefore hostile to liberty, ought to be exercised only within the narrowest bounds, in order to leave democracy free to develop itself without interference in its true social, intellectual, and economical strength. Unlike Jefferson and the Virginians, Gallatin never hesitated to claim for government all the powers necessary for whatever object was in hand; but he agreed with them in checking the practical use of power, and this he did with a degree of rigor which has been often imitated but never equalled. The Pennsylvanians followed Gallatin's teachings. They indulged in endless factiousness over offices, but they never attempted to govern, and after one brief experience they never rebelled. Thus holding abstract politics at arm's length, they supported the national government with a sagacious sense that their own interests were those of the United States.

Although the State was held by the New Englanders and Virginians in no high repute for quickness of intellect, Philadelphia in 1800 was still the intellectual centre of the nation. For ten years the city had been the seat of national government, and at the close of that period had gathered a more agreeable society, fashionable, literary, and political, than could be found anywhere, except in a few capital cities of Europe. This Quaker city of an ultra-democratic State startled travellers used to luxury, by its extravagance and display. According to the Duc de Liancourt, writing in 1797,—

"The profusion and luxury of Philadelphia on great days, at the tables of the wealthy, in their equipages, and the dresses of their wives and daughters, are extreme. I have seen balls on the President's birthday where the splendor of the rooms and the variety and richness of the dresses did not suffer in comparison with Europe; and it must be acknowledged that the beauty of the American ladies has the advantage in the comparison. The young women of Philadelphia are accomplished in different degrees, but beauty is general with them. They want the ease and fashion of French women, but the brilliancy of their complexion is infinitely superior. Even when they grow old they are still handsome; and it would be no exaggeration to say, in the numerous assemblies of Philadelphia it is impossible to meet with what is called a plain woman. As to the young men, they for the most part seem to belong to another species."

For ten years Philadelphia had attracted nearly all the intelligence and cultivation that could be detached from their native stocks. Stagnation was impossible in this rapid current of men and ideas. The Philadelphia press showed the effect of such unusual movement. There Cobbett vociferated libels against democrats. His career was cut short by a blunder of his own; for he quitted the safe field of politics in order to libel the physicians, and although medical practice was not much better than when it had been satirized by Le Sage some eighty years before, the physicians had not become less sensitive. If ever medical practice deserved to be libelled, the bleeding which was the common treatment not only for fevers but for consumption, and even for old age, warranted all that could be said against it; but Cobbett found to his cost that the Pennsylvanians were glad to bleed, or at least to seize the opportunity for silencing the libeller. In 1800 he returned to England; but the style of political warfare in which he was so great a master was already established in the Philadelphia press. An Irish-American named Duane, who had been driven from England and India for expressing opinions too liberal for the time and place, came to Philadelphia and took charge of the opposition newspaper, the "Aurora," which became in his hands the most energetic and slanderous paper in America. In the small society of the time libels rankled, and Duane rivalled Cobbett in the boldness with which he slandered. Another point of resemblance existed between the two men. At a later stage in his career Duane, like Cobbett, disregarded friend as well as foe; he then attacked all who offended him, and denounced his party leaders as bitterly as he did his opponents; but down to the year 1800 he reserved his abuse for his enemies, and the "Aurora" was the nearest approach to a modern newspaper to be found in the country.

Judged by the accounts of his more reputable enemies, Duane seemed beneath forbearance; but his sins, gross as they were, found abettors in places where such conduct was less to be excused. He was a scurrilous libeller; but so was Cobbett; so was William Coleman, who in 1801 became editor of the New York "Evening Post" under the eye of Alexander Hamilton; so was the refined Joseph Dennie, who in the same year established at Philadelphia the "Portfolio," a weekly paper devoted to literature, in which for years to come he was to write literary essays, diversified by slander of Jefferson. Perhaps none of these habitual libellers deserved censure so much as Fisher Ames, the idol of respectability, who cheered on his party to vituperate his political opponents. He saw no harm in showing "the knaves," Jefferson and Gallatin, "the cold-thinking villains who lead, 'whose black blood runs temperately bad,'" the motives of "their own base hearts.... The vain, the timid, and trimming must be made by examples to see that scorn smites and blasts and withers like lightning the knaves that mislead them." Little difference could be seen between the two parties in their use of such weapons, except that democrats claimed a right to slander opponents because they were monarchists and aristocrats, while Federalists thought themselves bound to smite and wither with scorn those who, as a class, did not respect established customs.

Of American newspapers there was no end; but the education supposed to have been widely spread by eighteenth-century newspapers was hardly to be distinguished from ignorance. The student of history might search forever these storehouses of political calumny for facts meant to instruct the public in any useful object. A few dozen advertisements of shipping and sales; a marine list; rarely or never a pricelist, unless it were European; copious extracts from English newspapers, and long columns of political disquisition,—such matter filled the chief city newspapers, from which the smaller sheets selected what their editors thought fit. Reporters and regular correspondents were unknown. Information of events other than political—the progress of the New York or Philadelphia water-works, of the Middlesex Canal, of Fitch's or Fulton's voyages, or even the commonest details of a Presidential inauguration—could rarely be found in the press. In such progress as newspapers had made Philadelphia took the lead, and in 1800 was at the height of her influence. Not until 1801 did the extreme Federalists set up the "Evening Post" under William Coleman, in New York, where at about the same time the Clinton interest put an English refugee named Cheetham in charge of their new paper, the "American Citizen and Watchtower," while Burr's friends established the "Morning Chronicle," edited by Dr. Peter Irving. Duane's importance was greatly reduced by this outburst of journalism in New York, and by the rise of the "National Intelligencer" at Washington, semi-official organ of Jefferson's administration. After the year 1800 the "Aurora" languished; but between 1795 and 1800 it was the leading newspaper of the United States, and boasted in 1802 of a circulation of four thousand copies, at least half of which its rivals declared to be imaginary.

Although Philadelphia was the literary as well as the political capital of America, nothing proved the existence of a highly intellectual society. When Joseph Dennie, a graduate of Harvard College, quitted Boston and established his "Portfolio" in Philadelphia in 1801, he complained as bitterly as the Pennsylvanian Cliffton against the land "where Genius sickens and where Fancy dies;" but he still thought Philadelphia more tolerable than any other city in the United States. With a little band of literary friends he passed his days in defying the indifference of his countrymen. "In the society of Mr. Dennie and his friends at Philadelphia I passed the few agreeable moments which my tour through the States afforded me," wrote in 1804 the British poet whom all the world united in calling by the familiar name of Tom Moore. "If I did not hate as I ought the rabble to which they are opposed, I could not value as I do the spirit with which they defy it; and in learning from them what Americans *can be*, I but see with the more indignation what Americans *are*."

> "Yet, yet forgive me, O you sacred few,
> Whom late by Delaware's green banks I knew;
> Whom, known and loved, through many a social eve
> 'T was bliss to live with, and 't was pain to leave.
> Oh, but for *such*, Columbia's days were done!
> Rank without ripeness, quickened without sun,
> Crude at the surface, rotten at the core,
> Her fruits would fall before her spring were o'er."

If Columbia's days were to depend on "*such*," they were scarcely worth prolonging; for Dennie's genius was but the thin echo of an English classicism thin at its best. Yet Moore's words had value, for they gave a lifelike idea of the "sacred few" who sat with him, drinking deep, and reviling America because she could not produce poets like Anacreon and artists like Phidias, and still more because Americans cared little for Addisonian essays. An adventurer called John Davis, who published in London a book of American travels, mentioned in it that he too met the Philadelphia authors. "Dennie passed his mornings in the shop of Mr. Dickens, which I found the rendezvous of the Philadelphia sons of literature,—Blair [Linn], author of a poem called the 'Powers of Genius;' Ingersoll, known by a tragedy of which I forget the title; Stock, celebrated for his dramatic criticisms." C. J. Ingersoll did in fact print a tragedy called "Edwy and Elgiva," which was acted in 1801, and John Blair Linn's "Powers of Genius" appeared in the same year; but Dennie's group boasted another member more notable than these. Charles Brockden Brown, the first American novelist of merit, was a Philadelphian. Davis called upon Brown. "He occupied a dismal room in a dismal street. I asked him whether a view of Nature would not be more propitious to composition, or whether he should not write with more facility were his window to command the prospect of the Lake of Geneva. 'Sir,' said he, 'good pens, thick paper, and ink well diluted would facilitate my composition more than the prospect of the broadest expanse of water or mountains rising against the clouds.'"

Pennsylvania was largely German and the Moravians were not without learning, yet no trace of German influence showed itself in the educated and literary class. Schiller was at the end of his career, and Goethe at the zenith of his powers; but neither was known in Pennsylvania, unless it might be by translations of the "Robbers" or the "Sorrows of Werther." As for deeper studies, search in America would be useless for what was rare or unknown either in England or France. Kant had closed and Hegel was beginning his labors; but the Western nations knew no more of German thought than of Egyptian hieroglyphics, and America had not yet reached the point of understanding that metaphysics apart from theology could exist at all. Locke was a college text-book, and possibly a few clergymen had learned to deride the idealism of Berkeley; but as an interest which concerned life, metaphysics, apart from Calvinism, had no existence in America, and was to have none for another generation. The literary labors of Americans followed easier paths, and such thought as prevailed was confined within a narrow field,—yet within this limit Pennsylvania had something to show, even though it failed to please the taste of Dennie and Moore.

Not far from the city of Philadelphia, on the banks of the Schuylkill, lived William Bartram, the naturalist, whose "Travels" through Florida and the Indian country, published in 1791, were once praised by Coleridge, and deserved reading both for the matter and the style. Not far from Bartram, and his best scholar, was Alexander Wilson, a Scotch poet of more than ordinary merit, gifted with a dogged enthusiasm, which in spite of obstacles gave to America an ornithology more creditable than anything yet accomplished in art or literature. Beyond the mountains, at Pittsburg, another author showed genuine and original qualities. American humor was not then so marked as it afterward became, and good-nature was rarer; but H. H. Brackenridge set an example of both in a book once universally popular throughout the South and West. A sort of prose "Hudibras," it had the merit of leaving no sting, for this satire on democracy was written by a democrat and published in the most democratic community of America. "Modern Chivalry" told the adventures of a militia captain, who riding about the country with a raw Irish servant, found this red-headed, ignorant bog-trotter, this Sancho Panza, a much more popular person than himself, who could only with difficulty be restrained from becoming a clergyman, an Indian chief, a member of the legislature, of the philosophical society, and of Congress. At length his employer got for him the appointment of excise officer in the Alleghanies, and was gratified at seeing him tarred and feathered by his democratic friends. "Modern Chivalry" was not only written in good last-century English, none too refined for its subject, but was more thoroughly American than any book yet published, or to be published until the "Letters of Major Jack Downing" and the "Georgia Scenes" of forty years later. Never known, even by title, in Europe, and little enjoyed in the seaboard States, where bog-trotters and weavers had no such prominence, Judge Brackenridge's book filled the place of Don Quixote on the banks of the Ohio and along the Mississippi.

Another man whose literary merits were not to be overlooked, had drifted to Philadelphia because of its varied attractions. If in the last century America could boast of a poet who shared some of the delicacy if not the grandeur of genius, it was Philip Freneau; whose verses, poured out for the occasion, ran freely, good and bad, but the bad, as was natural, much more freely than the good. Freneau proved his merit by an experience unique in history. He was twice robbed by the greatest English poets of his day. Among his many slight verses were some pleasing lines called "The Indian Burying Ground":—

"His bow for action ready bent,
    And arrows with a head of stone,
Can only mean that life is spent,
    And not the finer essence gone.

"By midnight moons, o'er moistening dews,
    In vestments for the chase arrayed,
The hunter still the deer pursues,
    The hunter and the deer,—a shade."

The last line was taken by the British poet Campbell for his own poem called "O'Connor's Child," and Freneau could afford to forgive the theft which thus called attention to the simple grace of his melody; but although one such compliment might fall to the lot of a common man, only merit could explain a second accident of the same kind. Freneau saw a greater genius than Campbell borrow from his modest capital. No one complained of Walter Scott for taking whatever he liked wherever he chose, to supply that flame of genius which quickened the world; but Freneau had the right to claim that Scott paid him the highest compliment one poet could pay to another. In the Introduction to the third canto of "Marmion" stood and still stands a line taken directly from the verse in Freneau's poem on the Heroes of Eutaw:—

"They took the spear—but left the shield."

All these men—Wilson, Brackenridge, Freneau—were democrats, and came not within the Federalist circle where Moore could alone see a hope for Columbia; yet the names of Federalists also survived in literature. Alexander Graydon's pleasant Memoirs could never lose interest. Many lawyers, clergymen, and physicians left lasting records. Dallas was bringing out his reports; Duponceau was laboring over jurisprudence and languages; William Lewis, William Rawle, and Judge Wilson were high authorities at the bar; Dr. Wistar was giving reputation to the Philadelphia Medical School, and the famous Dr. Physic was beginning to attract patients from far and near as the best surgeon in America. Gilbert Stuart, the best painter in the country, came to Philadelphia, and there painted portraits equal to the best that England or France could produce,—for Reynolds and Gainsborough were dead, and Sir Thomas Lawrence ruled the fashion of the time. If Franklin and Rittenhouse no longer lived to give scientific fame to Philadelphia, their liberal and scientific spirit survived. The reputation of the city was not confined to America, and the accident that made a Philadelphian, Benjamin West, President of the Royal Academy in succession to Sir Joshua Reynolds, was a tacit compliment, not undeserved, to the character of the American metropolis.

There manners were milder and more humane than elsewhere. Societies existed for lessening the hardships of the unfortunate. A society labored for the abolition of slavery without exciting popular passion, although New York contained more than twenty thousand slaves, and New Jersey more than twelve thousand. A society for alleviating the miseries of prisons watched the progress of experiments in the model jail, which stood alone of its kind in America. Elsewhere the treatment of criminals was such as it had ever been. In Connecticut they were still confined under-ground, in the shafts of an abandoned copper-mine. The Memoirs of Stephen Burroughs gave some idea of the prisons and prison discipline of Massachusetts. The Pennsylvania Hospital was also a model, for it contained a department for the insane, the only one of the sort in America except the Virginia Lunatic Asylum at Williamsburg. Even there the treatment of these beings, whom a later instinct of humanity thought peculiarly worthy of care and lavish expenditure, was harsh enough,—strait-jackets, whippings, chains, and dark-rooms being a part of the prescribed treatment in every such hospital in the world; but where no hospitals existed, as in New England, New York, and elsewhere, the treatment was apt to be far worse. No horror of the Middle Ages wrung the modern conscience with a sense of disgust more acute than was felt in remembering the treatment of the insane even within recent times. Shut in attics or cellars, or in cages outside a house, without warmth, light, or care, they lived in filth, with nourishment such as was thrown to dogs. Philadelphia led the way in humanitarian efforts which relieved man from incessant contact with these cruel and coarsening associations.

The depth of gratitude due to Pennsylvania as the model democratic society of the world was so great as to risk overestimating what had been actually done. As yet no commonschool system existed. Academies and colleges were indifferent. New Jersey was no better provided than Pennsylvania. The Englishman Weld, a keen if not a friendly critic, visited Princeton,—

"A large college," he said, "held in much repute by the neighboring States. The number of students amounts to upwards of seventy; from their appearance, however, and the course of studies they seem to be engaged in, like all the other American colleges I ever saw, it better deserves the title of a grammar-school than of a college. The library which we were shown is most wretched, consisting for the most part of old theological books not even arranged with any regularity. An orrery contrived by Mr. Rittenhouse stands at one end of the apartment, but it is quite out of repair, as well as a few detached parts of a philosophical apparatus enclosed in the same glass-case. At the opposite end of the room are two small cupboards which are shown as the museum. These contain a couple of small stuffed alligators and a few singular fishes in a miserable state of preservation, from their being repeatedly tossed about."

Philadelphia made no claim to a wide range of intellectual interests. As late as 1811, Latrobe, by education an architect and by genius an artist, wrote to Volney in France,—

"Thinking only of the profession and of the affluence which it yields in Europe to all who follow it, you forget that I am an engineer in America; that I am neither a mechanic nor a merchant, nor a planter of cotton, rice, or tobacco. You forget—for you know it as well as I do—

that with us the labor of the hand has precedence over that of the mind; that an engineer is considered only as an overseer of men who dig, and an architect as one that watches others who hew stone or wood."

The labor of the hand had precedence over that of the mind throughout the United States. If this was true in the city of Franklin, Rittenhouse, and West, the traveller who wandered farther toward the south felt still more strongly the want of intellectual variety, and found more cause for complaint.

Intellect of the Southern States

BETWEEN Pennsylvania and Virginia stretched no barrier of mountains or deserts. Nature seemed to mean that the northern State should reach toward the Chesapeake, and embrace its wide system of coasts and rivers. The Susquehanna, crossing Pennsylvania from north to south, rolled down wealth which in a few years built the city of Baltimore by the surplus of Pennsylvania's resources. Any part of Chesapeake Bay, or of the streams which flowed into it, was more easily accessible to Baltimore than any part of Massachusetts or Pennsylvania to New York. Every geographical reason argued that the Susquehanna, the Potomac, and the James should support one homogeneous people; yet the intellectual difference between Pennsylvania and Virginia was already more sharply marked than that between New England and the Middle States.

The old Virginia society was still erect, priding itself on its resemblance to the society of England, which had produced Hampden and Chatham. The Virginia gentleman, wherever met, was a country gentleman or a lawyer among a society of planters. The absence of city life was the sharpest characteristic of Virginia, even compared with South Carolina. In the best and greatest of Virginians, the virtues which always stood in most prominence were those of the field and farm,—the simple and straightforward mind, the notions of courage and truth, the absence of mercantile sharpness and quickness, the rusticity and open-handed hospitality, which could exist only where the

struggle for life was hardly a struggle at all. No visitor could resist the charm of kindly sympathy which softened the asperities
of Virginian ambition. Whether young Albert Gallatin went
there, hesitating between Europe and America, or the still
younger William Ellery Channing, with all New England on
his active conscience, the effect was the same:—

"I blush for my own people," wrote Channing from
Richmond in 1799, "when I compare the selfish prudence
of a Yankee with the generous confidence of a Virginian.
Here I find great vices, but greater virtues than I left behind me. There is one single trait which attaches me to
the people I live with more than all the virtues of New
England,—they *love money less* than we do; they are more
disinterested; their patriotism is not tied to their purse-
strings. Could I only take from the Virginians their sen-
suality and their slaves, I should think them the greatest
people in the world. As it is, with a few great virtues, they
have innumerable vices."

Even forty years afterward, so typical a New Englander as the
poet Bryant acknowledged that "whatever may be the comparison in other respects, the South certainly has the advantage over
us in point of manners." Manners were not all their charm; for
the Virginians at the close of the eighteenth century were inferior
to no class of Americans in the sort of education then supposed
to make refinement. The Duc de Liancourt bore witness:—

"In spite of the Virginian love for dissipation, the taste
for reading is commoner there among men of the first
class than in any other part of America; but the populace
is perhaps more ignorant there than elsewhere."

Those whom Liancourt called "men of the first class" were

equal to any standard of excellence known to history. Their range was narrow, but within it they were supreme. The traditions of high breeding were still maintained, and a small England, much as it existed in the time of the Commonwealth, was perpetuated in the Virginia of 1800. Social position was a birthright, not merely of the well born, but of the highly gifted. Nearly all the great lawyers of Virginia were of the same social stock as in New England,—poor and gifted men, welcomed into a landed aristocracy simple in tastes and genial in temper. Chief-Justice Marshall was such a man, commanding respect and regard wherever he was seen,—perhaps most of all from New Englanders, who were least familiar with the type. George Mason was an ideal republican,—a character as strong in its way as Washington or Marshall. George Wythe the Chancellor stood in the same universal esteem; and even his young clerk Henry Clay, "the mill-boy of the slashes," who had lately left Chancellor Wythe's office to set up one of his own at Lexington in Kentucky, inherited that Virginia geniality which, as it ripened with his years, made him an idol among Northern and Western multitudes who knew neither the source nor secret of his charm. Law and politics were the only objects of Virginian thought; but within these bounds the Virginians achieved triumphs. What could America offer in legal literature that rivalled the judicial opinions of Chief-Justice Marshall? What political essay equalled the severe beauty of George Mason's Virginia Bill of Rights? What single production of an American pen reached the fame of Thomas Jefferson's Declaration of Independence? "The Virginians are the best orators I ever heard," wrote the young Channing; although Patrick Henry, the greatest of them all, was no longer alive.

Every one admitted that Virginia society was ill at ease. In colonial days it rested on a few great props, the strongest being its close connection with England; and after this had been cut away by the Revolutionary War, primogeniture, the Church, exemption of land from seizure for debt, and negro slavery remained to support the oligarchy of planters. The momentum given by the Declaration of Independence enabled Jefferson and George Wythe to sweep primogeniture from the statute book. After an interval of several years, Madison carried the law which severed Church from State. There the movement ended. All the great Virginians would gladly have gone on, but the current began to flow against them. They suggested a bill for emancipation, but could find no one to father it in the legislature, and they shrank from the storm it would excite.

President Washington, in 1796, in a letter already quoted, admitted that land in Virginia was lower in price than land of the same quality in Pennsylvania. For this inferiority he suggested, among other reasons, the explanation that Pennsylvania had made laws for the gradual abolition of slavery, and he declared nothing more certain than that Virginia must adopt similar laws at a period not remote. Had the Virginians seen a sure prospect that such a step would improve their situation, they would probably have taken it; but the slave-owners were little pleased at the results of reforms already effected, and they were in no humor for abolishing more of their old institutions. The effects of disestablishing the Church were calculated to disgust them with all reform. From early times the colony had been divided into parishes, and each parish owned a church building. The system was the counterpart of that established in New England. The church lands, glebes, and endowments were administered by the clergyman, wardens, and vestry. Good society in Virginia recognized no other religion than was taught in this branch of English episcopacy. "Sure I am of one thing," was the remark in the Virginia legislature of an old-fashioned Federalist, with powdered hair, three-cornered hat, long queue, and white top-boots,—"Sure I am of one thing, that no *gentleman* would choose any road to heaven but the Episcopal." Every plantation was attached to a parish, and the earliest associations of every well-bred man and woman in Virginia were connected with the Church service. In spite of all this, no sooner had Madison and his friends taken away the support of the State than the Church perished. They argued that freedom of religion worked well in Pennsylvania, and therefore must succeed in Virginia; but they were wrong. The Virginia gentry stood by and saw their churches closed, the roofs rot, the aisles and pews become a refuge for sheep and foxes, the tombstones of their ancestry built into strange walls or turned into flagging to be worn by the feet of slaves. By the year 1800, Bishop Madison found his diocese left so nearly bare of clergy and communicants that after a few feeble efforts to revive interest he abandoned the struggle, and contented himself with the humbler task of educating boys at the ancient College of William and Mary in the deserted colonial capital of Williamsburg. There the English traveller Weld visited him about the year 1797, and gave a curious picture of his establishment:—

"The Bishop," he said, "is president of the college, and has apartments in the buildings. Half-a-dozen or more of the students, the eldest about twelve years old, dined at his table one day that I was there. Some were without shoes or stockings, others without coats. During dinner they constantly rose to help themselves at the sideboard. A couple of dishes of salted meat and some oyster-soup formed the whole of the dinner."

Such a state of society was picturesque, but not encouraging. An aristocracy so lacking in energy and self-confidence was a mere shell, to be crushed, as one might think, by a single vigorous blow. Nevertheless, Jefferson and Madison, after striking it again and again with the full force of Revolutionary violence, were obliged to desist, and turned their reforming axes against the Church and hierarchy of New England. There they could do nothing but good, for the society of New England was sound, whatever became of the Church or of slavery; but in Virginia the gap which divided gentry from populace was enormous; and another gap, which seemed impassable, divided the populace from the slaves. Jefferson's reforms crippled and impoverished the gentry, but did little for the people, and for the slaves nothing.

Nowhere in America existed better human material than in the middle and lower classes of Virginians. As explorers, adventurers, fighters,—wherever courage, activity, and force were wanted,—they had no equals; but they had never known discipline, and were beyond measure jealous of restraint. With all their natural virtues and indefinite capacities for good, they were rough and uneducated to a degree that shocked their own native leaders. Jefferson tried in vain to persuade them that they needed schools. Their character was stereotyped, and development impossible; for even Jefferson, with all his liberality of ideas, was Virginian enough to discourage the introduction of manufactures and the gathering of masses in cities, without which no new life could grow. Among the common people, intellectual activity was confined to hereditary commonplaces of politics, resting on the axiom that Virginia was the typical society of a future Arcadian America. To escape the tyranny of Cæsar by perpetuating the simple and isolated lives of their fathers was the sum of their political philosophy; to fix upon the national government the stamp of their own idyllic conservatism was the height of their ambition.

Debarred from manufactures, possessed of no shipping, and enjoying no domestic market, Virginian energies necessarily knew no other resource than agriculture. Without church, university, schools, or literature in any form that required or fostered intellectual life, the Virginians concentrated their thoughts almost exclusively upon politics; and this concentration produced a result so distinct and lasting, and in character so respectable, that American history would lose no small part of its interest in losing the Virginia school.

No one denied that Virginia, like Massachusetts, in the War of Independence, believed herself competent to follow independently of other provinces whatever path seemed good. The Constitution of Virginia did not, like that of Massachusetts, authorize the governor to "be the commander-in-chief of the army and navy," in order "to take and surprise, by all ways and means whatsoever, all and every such person or persons (with their ships, arms, ammunition, and other goods) as shall in a hostile manner invade or attempt the invading, conquering, or annoying this Commonwealth;" but although Massachusetts expressed the power in language more detailed, Virginia held to its essence with equal tenacity. When experience showed the necessity of "creating a more perfect union," none of the great States were unanimous for the change. Massachusetts and New York were with difficulty induced to accept the Constitution of 1787. Their final assent was wrung from them by the influence of the cities and of the commercial class; but Virginia contained no cities and few merchants. The majority by which the State Convention of Virginia, after an obstinate contest, adopted the Constitution, was influenced by pure patriotism as far as any political influence could be called pure; but the popular majority was probably hostile to the Constitution, and certainly remained hostile to the exercise of its powers. From the first the State took an attitude of opposition to the national government, which became more and more decided, until in 1798 it found expression in a formal announcement, through the legislature and governor, that the limit of further obedience was at hand. The General Assembly adopted Resolutions promising support to the government of the United States in all measures warranted by the Constitution, but declaring the powers of the federal government "no further valid than they are authorized by the grants enumerated in that compact; and that in case of a deliberate, palpable, and dangerous exercise of other powers, not granted by said compact, the States who are parties thereto have the right, and are in duty bound, to interpose, for arresting the progress of the evil and for maintaining within their respective limits the authorities, rights, and liberties appertaining to them."

Acting immediately on this view, the General Assembly did interpose by declaring certain laws, known as the Alien and Sedition Laws, unconstitutional, and by inviting the other States to concur, in confidence "that the necessary and proper measures will be taken by each for co-operating with this State in maintaining unimpaired the authorities, rights, and liberties reserved to the States respectively or to the people."

These Virginia Resolutions, which were drawn by Madison, seemed strong enough to meet any possible aggression from the national government; but Jefferson, as though not quite satisfied with these, recommended the Kentucky legislature to adopt still stronger. The draft of the Kentucky Resolutions, whether originally composed or only approved by him, representing certainly his own convictions, declared that "where powers are assumed which have not been delegated a nullification of the Act is the rightful remedy," and "that every State has a natural right, in cases not within the compact, to nullify of their own authority all assumptions of power by others within their limits." Jefferson did not doubt "that the co-States, recurring to their natural right in cases not made federal, will concur in declaring these acts void and of no force, and will each take measures of its own for providing that neither these acts, nor any others of the federal government not plainly and intentionally authorized by the Constitution, shall be exercised within their respective territories."

In the history of Virginia thought, the personal opinions of Jefferson and Madison were more interesting, if not more important, than the official opinion of State legislatures. Kentucky shrank from using language which seemed unnecessarily violent, but still declared, with all the emphasis needed, that the national government was not "the exclusive or final judge of the extent of the powers delegated to itself, since that would have made its discretion, and not the Constitution, the measure of its powers," but that each party had an equal right to judge for itself as to an infraction of the compact, and the proper redress; that in the case of the Alien and Sedition Laws the compact had been infringed, and that these Acts, being unconstitutional and therefore void, "may tend to drive these States into revolution and blood;" finally, the State of Kentucky called for an expression of sentiment from other States, like Virginia not doubting "that the co-States, recurring to their natural right in cases not made federal, will concur in declaring these Acts void and of no force."

These famous Resolutions of Virginia and Kentucky, historically the most interesting of all the intellectual products of the Virginia school, were adopted in 1798 and 1799. In 1800, Jefferson their chief author was chosen President of the United States, and Madison became his Secretary of State. Much discussion then and afterward arose over the Constitutional theory laid down by Virginia and Kentucky, and thus apparently adopted by the Union; but in such cases of disputed powers that theory was soundest which was backed by the strongest force, for the sanction of force was the most necessary part of law. The United States government was at that time powerless to enforce its theories; while, on the other hand, Virginia had all the power necessary for the object desired. The Republican leaders believed that the State was at liberty to withdraw from the Union if it should think that an infraction of the Constitution had taken place; and Jefferson in 1798 preferred to go on by way of Resolution rather than by way of Secession, not because of any doubt as to the right, but because, "if we now reduce our Union to Virginia and North Carolina, immediately the conflict will be established between those two States, and they will end by breaking into their simple units." In other letters he explained that the Kentucky Resolutions were intended "to leave the matter in such a train as that we may not be committed absolutely to push the matter to extremities, and yet may be free to push as far as events will render prudent." Union was a question of expediency, not of obligation. This was the conviction of the true Virginia school, and of Jefferson's opponents as well as his supporters; of Patrick Henry, as well as John Taylor of Caroline and John Randolph of Roanoke.

The Virginia and Kentucky Resolutions, giving form to ideas that had not till then been so well expressed, left a permanent mark in history, and fixed for an indefinite time the direction and bounds of Virginia politics; but if New England could go no further in the lines of thought pursued by Fisher Ames and Timothy Dwight, Virginia could certainly expect no better results from those defined by Jefferson and Madison. The science of politics, if limited by the Resolutions of Virginia and Kentucky, must degenerate into an enumeration of powers reserved from exercise. Thought could find little room for free development where it confined its action to narrowing its own field.

This tendency of the Virginia school was the more remarkable because it seemed little suited to the tastes and instincts of the two men who gave it expression and guided its course. By common consent Thomas Jefferson was its intellectual leader. According to the admitted standards of greatness, Jefferson was a great man. After all deductions on which his enemies might choose to insist, his character could not be denied elevation, versatility, breadth, insight, and delicacy; but neither as a politician nor as a political philosopher did he seem at ease in the atmosphere which surrounded him. As a leader of democracy he appeared singularly out of place. As reserved as President Washington in the face of popular familiarities, he never showed himself in crowds. During the last thirty years of his life he was not seen in a Northern city, even during his Presidency; nor indeed was he seen at all except on horseback, or by his friends and visitors in his own house. With manners apparently popular and informal, he led a life of his own, and allowed few persons to share it. His tastes were for that day excessively refined. His instincts were those of a liberal European nobleman, like the Duc de Liancourt, and he built for himself at Monticello a château above contact with man. The rawness of political life was an incessant torture to him, and personal attacks made him keenly unhappy. His true delight was in an intellectual life of science and art. To read, write, speculate in new lines of thought, to keep abreast of the intellect of Europe, and to feed upon Homer and Horace, were pleasures more to his mind than any to be found in a public assembly. He had some knowledge of mathematics, and a little acquaintance with classical art; but he fairly revelled in what he believed to be beautiful, and his writings often betrayed subtile feeling for artistic form,—a sure mark of intellectual sensuousness. He shrank from whatever was rough or coarse, and his yearning for sympathy was almost feminine. That such a man should have ventured upon the stormy ocean of politics was surprising, the more because he was no orator, and owed nothing to any magnetic influence of voice or person. Never effective in debate, for seventeen years before his Presidency he had not appeared in a legislative body except in the chair of the Senate. He felt a nervous horror for the contentiousness of such assemblies, and even among his own friends he sometimes abandoned for the moment his strongest convictions rather than support them by an effort of authority.

If Jefferson appeared ill at ease in the position of a popular leader, he seemed equally awkward in the intellectual restraints of his own political principles. His mind shared little in common with the provincialism on which the Virginia and Kentucky Resolutions were founded. His instincts led him to widen rather than to narrow the bounds of every intellectual exercise; and if vested with political authority, he could no more resist the temptation to stretch his powers than he could abstain from using his mind on any subject merely because he might be drawn upon ground supposed to be dangerous. He was a deist, believing that men could manage their own salvation without the help of a state church. Prone to innovation, he sometimes generalized without careful analysis. He was a theorist, prepared to risk the fate of mankind on the chance of reasoning far from certain in its details. His temperament was sunny and sanguine, and the atrabilious philosophy of New England was intolerable to him. He was curiously vulnerable, for he seldom wrote a page without exposing himself to attack. He was superficial in his knowledge, and a martyr to the disease of omniscience. Ridicule of his opinions and of himself was an easy task, in which his Federalist opponents delighted, for his English was often confused, his assertions inaccurate, and at times of excitement he was apt to talk with indiscretion; while with all his extraordinary versatility of character and opinions, he seemed during his entire life to breathe with perfect satisfaction nowhere except in the liberal, literary, and scientific air of Paris in 1789.

Jefferson aspired beyond the ambition of a nationality, and embraced in his view the whole future of man. That the United States should become a nation like France, England, or Russia, should conquer the world like Rome, or develop a typical race like the Chinese, was no part of his scheme. He wished to begin a new era. Hoping for a time when the world's ruling interests should cease to be local and should become universal; when questions of boundary and nationality should become insignificant; when armies and navies should be reduced to the work of police, and politics should consist only in non-intervention,—he set himself to the task of governing, with this golden age in view. Few men have dared to legislate as though eternal peace were at hand, in a world torn by wars and convulsions and drowned in blood; but this was what Jefferson aspired to do. Even in such dangers, he believed that Americans might safely set an example which the Christian world should be led by interest to respect and at length to imitate. As he conceived a true American policy, war was a blunder, an unnecessary risk; and even in case of robbery and aggression the United States, he believed, had only to stand on the defensive in order to obtain justice in the end. He would not consent to build up a new nationality merely to create more navies and armies, to perpetuate the crimes and follies of Europe; the central government at Washington should not be permitted to indulge in the miserable ambitions that had made the Old World a hell, and frustrated the hopes of humanity.

With these humanitarian ideas which passed beyond the bounds of nationality, Jefferson held other views which seemed narrower than ordinary provincialism. Cities, manufactures, mines, shipping, and accumulation of capital led, in his opinion, to corruption and tyranny.

> "Generally speaking," said he, in his only elaborate work, the Notes on Virginia, "the proportion which the aggregate of the other classes of citizens bears in any State to that of its husbandmen is the proportion of its unsound to its healthy parts, and is a good enough barometer whereby to measure its degree of corruption. . . . Those who labor in the earth are the chosen people of God if ever he had a chosen people, whose breasts he has made his peculiar deposit for substantial and genuine virtue."

This doctrine was not original with Jefferson, but its application to national affairs on a great scale was something new in the world, and the theory itself clashed with his intellectual instincts of liberality and innovation.

A school of political thought, starting with postulates like these, was an interesting study, and would have been more interesting had Jefferson's friends undertaken to develop his ideas in the extent he held them. Perhaps this was impossible. At all events, Madison, although author of the Virginia Resolutions, showed little earnestness in carrying out their principles either as a political or as a literary task; and John Taylor of Caroline, the only consistent representative of the school, began his writings only when political power had established precedents inconsistent with their object.

With such simple conceptions as their experience gave them in politics, law, and agriculture, the Virginians appeared to be satisfied; and whether satisfied or not, they were for the time helpless to produce other literature, science, or art. From the three States lying farther south, no greater intellectual variety could be expected. In some respects North Carolina, though modest in ambition and backward in thought, was still the healthiest community south of the Potomac. Neither aristocratic like Virginia and South Carolina, nor turbulent like Georgia, nor troubled by a sense of social importance, but above all thoroughly democratic, North Carolina tolerated more freedom of political action and showed less family and social influence, fewer vested rights in political power, and less tyranny of slaveholding interests and terrors than were common elsewhere in the South. Neither cultivated nor brilliant in intellect, nor great in thought, industry, energy, or organization, North Carolina was still interesting and respectable. The best qualities of the State were typified in its favorite representative, Nathaniel Macon.

The small society of rice and cotton planters at Charleston, with their cultivated tastes and hospitable habits, delighted in whatever reminded them of European civilization. They were travellers, readers, and scholars; the society of Charleston compared well in refinement with that of any city of its size in the world, and English visitors long thought it the most agreeable in America. In the southern wilderness which stretched from the Appomattox to the St. Mary's, Charleston was the only oasis. The South Carolinians were ambitious for other distinctions than those which could be earned at the bar or on the plantation. From there Washington Allston went to study at Harvard College, and after taking his degree in the same class with young Buckminster, sailed in the same year, 1800, for Europe with his friend Malbone, to learn to express in color and form the grace and dignity of his imagination. In South Carolina were felt the instincts of city life. During two or three weeks of the winter, the succession of dinners, balls, and races at Charleston rivalled the gayety of Philadelphia itself; and although the city was dull during the rest of the year, it was not deserted even in the heat of summer, for the sea-breeze made it a watering-place, like Boston, and the deadly fevers sure to kill the white man who should pass a night on one bank of the Ashley River were almost unknown on the other. In the summer, therefore, the residents remained or returned; the children got their schooling, and business continued. For this reason South Carolina knew less of the country hospitality which made Virginia famous; city life had the larger share in existence, although in the hot weather torpor and languor took the place of gayety. In certain respects Charleston was more Northern in habits than any town of the North. In other warm countries, the summer evening was commonly the moment when life was best worth living; music, love-making, laughter, and talk turned night into day; but Charleston was Puritanic in discipline. Every night at ten o'clock the slamming of window-blinds and locking of doors warned strangers and visitors to go not only to their houses, but to their beds. The citizens looked with contempt on the gayety of Spanish or Italian temper. Beneath all other thoughts, the care of the huge slave population remained constant. The streets were abandoned at an early hour to the patrol, and no New England village was more silent.

Confident as the Carolinian was in the strength of the slave-system, and careless as he seemed and thought himself to be on that account, the recent fate of St. Domingo gave him cause for constant anxiety; but even without anxiety, he would have been grave. The gentry of the lower country belonged to the same English class which produced the gentry of Virginia and Massachusetts. The austerity of the Puritan may have been an exaggerated trait, but among the Middletons, Pinckneys, Rutledges, and Lowndeses the seriousness of the original English stock was also not without effect in the habit of their minds. They showed it in their treatment of the slave-system, but equally in their churches and houses, their occupations and prejudices, their races and sports, the character of their entertainments, the books they read, and the talk at their tables. No gentleman belonged to any church but the Anglican, or connected himself with trade. No court departed from the practice and precedents of English law, however anomalous they might be. Before the Revolution large numbers of young men had been educated in England, and their influence was still strong in the society of Charleston. The younger generation inherited similar tastes. Of this class the best-known name which will appear in this narrative was that of William Lowndes; and no better example could be offered of the serious temper which marked Carolinian thought, than was given by the career of this refined and highly educated gentleman, almost the last of his school.

Charleston was more cosmopolitan than any part of Virginia, and enjoyed also a certain literary reputation on account of David Ramsay, whose works were widely read; and of Governor Drayton, whose "Letters written during a Tour through the Northern and Eastern States," and "View of South Carolina," gave an idea of the author as well as of the countries he described. Charleston also possessed a library of three or four thousand well-selected books, and maintained a well-managed theatre. The churches were almost as strictly attended as those in Boston. The fashionable wine-party was even more common, and perhaps the guests took pride in drinking deeper than they would have been required to do in New York or Philadelphia.

Politics had not mastered the thought of South Carolina so completely as that of Virginia, and the natural instincts of Carolinian society should have led the gentry to make common cause with the gentry of New England and the Middle States against democratic innovations. The conservative side in politics seemed to be that which no Carolinian gentleman could fail to support. The oligarchy of South Carolina, in defiance of democratic principles, held the political power of the State, and its interests could never harmonize with those of a theoretic democracy, or safely consent to trust the national government in the hands of Jefferson and his friends, who had founded their power by breaking down in Virginia an oligarchy closely resembling that of the Carolinian rice-planters. Yet in 1800 enough of these gentlemen, under the lead of Charles Pinckney, deserted their Northern friends, to secure the defeat of the Federalist candidates, and to elect Jefferson as President. For this action, no satisfactory reason was ever given. Of all States in the Union, South Carolina, under its actual system of politics, was the last which could be suspected of democratic tendencies.

Such want of consistency seemed to show some peculiarity of character. Not every educated and privileged class has sacrificed itself to a social sentiment, least of all without understanding its object. The eccentricity was complicated by another peculiar element of society. In South Carolina the interesting union between English tastes and provincial prejudices, which characterized the wealthy planters of the coast, was made more striking by contrast with the character of the

poor and hardy yeomanry of the upper country. The seriousness of Charleston society changed to severity in the mountains. Rude, ignorant, and in some of its habits half barbarous,
this population, in the stiffness of its religious and social expression, resembled the New England of a century before
rather than the liberality of the Union. Largely settled by
Scotch and Irish emigrants, with the rigid Presbyterian doctrine and conservatism of their class, they were democratic in
practice beyond all American democrats, and were more conservative in thought than the most aristocratic Europeans.
Though sharply divided both socially and by interest from the
sea-coast planters, these up-country farmers had one intellectual sympathy with their fellow-citizens in Charleston,—a
sympathy resting on their common dislike for change, on the
serious element which lay at the root of their common charac-
ters; and this marriage of two widely divergent minds produced
one of the most extraordinary statesmen of America. In the
year 1800 John Caldwell Calhoun, a boy of eighteen, went
from the upper country to his brother-in-law's academy in
Georgia. Grown nearly to manhood without contact with the
world, his modes of thought were those of a Connecticut
Calvinist; his mind was cold, stern, and metaphysical; but he
had the energy and ambition of youth, the political fervor of
Jeffersonian democracy, and little sympathy with slavery or
slave-owners. At this early age he, like many other Republicans,
looked on slavery as a "scaffolding," to be taken down when the
building should be complete. A radical democrat, less liberal,
less cultivated, and much less genial than Jefferson, Calhoun
was the true heir to his intellectual succession; stronger in logic,
bolder in action. Upon him was to fall the duty of attempting
to find for Carolina an escape from the logical conclusions of
those democratic principles which Jefferson in 1800 claimed for
his own, but which in the full swing of his power, and to the
last day of his life, he shrank from pressing to their results.

Viewed from every side by which it could be approached, the society of South Carolina, more than that of any other portion of the Union, seemed to bristle with contradictions. The elements of intellectual life existed without a sufficient intellectual atmosphere. Society, colonial by origin and dependent by the conditions of its existence, was striving to exist without external support. Whether it would stand or fall, and whether, either standing or falling, it could contribute any new element to American thought, were riddles which, with so many others, American history was to answer.

American Ideals

NEARLY every foreign traveller who visited the United States during these early years, carried away an impression sober if not sad. A thousand miles of desolate and dreary forest, broken here and there by settlements; along the seacoast a few flourishing towns devoted to commerce; no arts, a provincial literature, a cancerous disease of negro slavery, and differences of political theory fortified within geographical lines,—what could be hoped for such a country except to repeat the story of violence and brutality which the world already knew by heart, until repetition for thousands of years had wearied and sickened mankind? Ages must probably pass before the interior could be thoroughly settled; even Jefferson, usually a sanguine man, talked of a thousand years with acquiescence, and in his first Inaugural Address, at a time when the Mississippi River formed the Western boundary, spoke of the country as having "room enough for our descendants to the hundredth and thousandth generation." No prudent person dared to act on the certainty that when settled, one government could comprehend the whole; and when the day of separation should arrive, and America should have her Prussia, Austria, and Italy, as she already had her England, France, and Spain, what else could follow but a return to the old conditions of local jealousies, wars, and corruption which had made a slaughter-house of Europe?

The mass of Americans were sanguine and self-confident, partly by temperament, but partly also by reason of ignorance;

for they knew little of the difficulties which surrounded a complex society. The Duc de Liancourt, like many critics, was struck by this trait. Among other instances, he met with one in the person of a Pennsylvania miller, Thomas Lea, "a sound American patriot, persuading himself that nothing good is done, and that no one has any brains, except in America; that the wit, the imagination, the genius of Europe are already in decrepitude;" and the duke added: "This error is to be found in almost all Americans,—legislators, administrators, as well as millers, and is less innocent there." In the year 1796 the House of Representatives debated whether to insert in the Reply to the President's Speech a passing remark that the nation was "the freest and most enlightened in the world,"—a nation as yet in swaddling-clothes, which had neither literature, arts, sciences, nor history; nor even enough nationality to be sure that it was a nation. The moment was peculiarly ill-chosen for such a claim, because Europe was on the verge of an outburst of genius. Goethe and Schiller, Mozart and Haydn, Kant and Fichte, Cavendish and Herschel were making way for Walter Scott, Wordsworth, and Shelley, Heine and Balzac, Beethoven and Hegel, Oersted and Cuvier, great physicists, biologists, geologists, chemists, mathematicians, metaphysicians, and historians by the score. Turner was painting his earliest landscapes, and Watt completing his latest steam-engine; Napoleon was taking command of the French armies, and Nelson of the English fleets; investigators, reformers, scholars, and philosophers swarmed, and the influence of enlightenment, even amid universal war, was working with an energy such as the world had never before conceived. The idea that Europe was in her decrepitude proved only ignorance and want of enlightenment, if not of freedom, on the part of Americans, who could only excuse their error by pleading that notwithstanding these objections, in matters which for the moment most concerned themselves Europe was a full century behind America. If they were right in thinking that the next necessity of human progress was to lift the average man upon an intellectual and social level with the most favored, they stood at least three generations nearer than Europe to their common goal. The destinies of the United States were certainly staked, without reserve or escape, on the soundness of this doubtful and even improbable principle, ignoring or overthrowing the institutions of church, aristocracy, family, army, and political intervention, which long experience had shown to be needed for the safety of society. Europe might be right in thinking that without such safeguards society must come to an end; but even Europeans must concede that there was a chance, if no greater than one in a thousand, that America might, at least for a time, succeed. If this stake of temporal and eternal welfare stood on the winning card; if man actually should become more virtuous and enlightened, by mere process of growth, without church or paternal authority; if the average human being could accustom himself to reason with the logical processes of Descartes and Newton!—what then?

Then, no one could deny that the United States would win a stake such as defied mathematics. With all the advantages of science and capital, Europe must be slower than America to reach the common goal. American society might be both sober and sad, but except for negro slavery it was sound and healthy in every part. Stripped for the hardest work, every muscle firm and elastic, every ounce of brain ready for use, and not a trace of superfluous flesh on his nervous and supple body, the American stood in the world a new order of man. From Maine to Florida, society was in this respect the same, and was so organized as to use its human forces with more economy than could be approached by any society of the world elsewhere. Not only were artificial barriers carefully removed, but every influence that could appeal to ordinary ambition was applied. No brain or appetite active enough to be conscious of stimulants could fail to answer the intense incentive. Few human beings, however sluggish, could long resist the temptation to acquire power; and the elements of power were to be had in America almost for the asking. Reversing the old-world system, the American stimulant increased in energy as it reached the lowest and most ignorant class, dragging and whirling them upward as in the blast of a furnace. The penniless and homeless Scotch or Irish immigrant was caught and consumed by it; for every stroke of the axe and the hoe made him a capitalist, and made gentlemen of his children. Wealth was the strongest agent for moving the mass of mankind; but political power was hardly less tempting to the more intelligent and better-educated swarms of American-born citizens, and the instinct of activity, once created, seemed heritable and permanent in the race.

Compared with this lithe young figure, Europe was actually in decrepitude. Mere class distinctions, the *patois* or dialect of the peasantry, the fixity of residence, the local costumes and habits marking a history that lost itself in the renewal of identical generations, raised from birth barriers which paralyzed half the population. Upon this mass of inert matter rested the Church and the State, holding down activity of thought. Endless wars withdrew many hundred thousand men from production, and changed them into agents of waste; huge debts, the evidence of past wars and bad government, created interests to support the system and fix its burdens on the laboring class; courts, with habits of extravagance that shamed common-sense, helped to consume private economies. All this might have been borne; but behind this stood aristocracies, sucking their nourishment from industry, producing nothing themselves, employing little or no active capital or intelligent labor, but pressing on the energies and ambition of society with the weight of an incubus. Picturesque and entertaining as these social anomalies were, they were better fitted for the theatre or for a museum of historical costumes than for an active workshop preparing to compete with such machinery as America would soon command. From an economical point of view, they were as incongruous as would have been the appearance of a mediæval knight in helmet and armor, with battle-axe and shield, to run the machinery of Arkwright's cotton-mill; but besides their bad economy they also tended to prevent the rest of society from gaining a knowledge of its own capacities. In Europe, the conservative habit of mind was fortified behind power. During nearly a century Voltaire himself—the friend of kings, the wit and poet, historian and philosopher of his age—had carried on, in daily terror, in exile and excommunication, a protest against an intellectual despotism contemptible even to its own supporters. Hardly was Voltaire dead, when Priestley, as great a man if not so great a wit, trying to do for England what Voltaire tried to do for France, was mobbed by the people of Birmingham and driven to America. Where Voltaire and Priestley failed, common men could not struggle; the weight of society stifled their thought. In America the balance between conservative and liberal forces was close; but in Europe conservatism held the physical power of government. In Boston a young Buckminster might be checked for a time by his father's prayers or commands in entering the path that led toward freer thought; but youth beckoned him on, and every reward that society could offer was dangled before his eyes. In London or Paris, Rome, Madrid, or Vienna, he must have sacrificed the worldly prospects of his life.

Granting that the American people were about to risk their future on a new experiment, they naturally wished to throw aside all burdens of which they could rid themselves. Believing that in the long run interest, not violence, would rule the world, and that the United States must depend for safety and success on the interests they could create, they were tempted to look upon war and preparations for war as the worst of blunders; for they were sure that every dollar capitalized in industry was a means of overthrowing their enemies more effective than a thousand dollars spent on frigates or standing armies. The success of the American system was, from this point of view, a question of economy. If they could relieve themselves from debts, taxes, armies, and government interference with industry, they must succeed in outstripping Europe in economy of production; and Americans were even then partly aware that if their machine were not so weakened by these economies as to break down in the working, it must of necessity break down every rival. If their theory was sound, when the day of competition should arrive, Europe might choose between American and Chinese institutions, but there would be no middle path; she might become a confederated democracy, or a wreck.

Whether these ideas were sound or weak, they seemed self-evident to those Northern democrats who, like Albert Gallatin, were comparatively free from slave-owning theories, and understood the practical forces of society. If Gallatin wished to reduce the interference of government to a minimum, and cut down expenditures to nothing, he aimed not so much at saving money as at using it with the most certain effect. The revolution of 1800 was in his eyes chiefly political, because it was social; but as a revolution of society, he and his friends hoped to make it the most radical that had occurred since the downfall of the Roman empire. Their ideas were not yet cleared by experience, and were confused by many contradictory prejudices, but wanted neither breadth nor shrewdness.

Many apparent inconsistencies grew from this undeveloped form of American thought, and gave rise to great confusion in the different estimates of American character that were made both at home and abroad.

That Americans should not be liked was natural; but that they should not be understood was more significant by far. After the downfall of the French republic they had no right to expect a kind word from Europe, and during the next twenty years they rarely received one. The liberal movement of Europe was cowed, and no one dared express democratic sympathies until the Napoleonic tempest had passed. With this attitude Americans had no right to find fault, for Europe cared less to injure them than to protect herself. Nevertheless, observant readers could not but feel surprised that none of the numerous Europeans who then wrote or spoke about America seemed to study the subject seriously. The ordinary traveller was apt to be little more reflective than a bee or an ant, but some of these critics possessed powers far from ordinary; yet Talleyrand alone showed that had he but seen America a few years later than he did, he might have suggested some sufficient reason for apparent contradictions that perplexed him in the national character. The other travellers—great and small, from the Duc de Liancourt to Basil Hall, a long and suggestive list—were equally perplexed. They agreed in observing the contradictions, but all, including Talleyrand, saw only sordid motives. Talleyrand expressed extreme astonishment at the apathy of Americans in the face of religious sectarians; but he explained it by assuming that the American ardor of the moment was absorbed in money-making. The explanation was evidently insufficient, for the Americans were capable of feeling and showing excitement, even to their great pecuniary injury, as they frequently proved; but in the foreigner's range of observation, love of money was the most conspicuous and most common trait of American character. "There is, perhaps, no civilized country in the world," wrote Félix de Beaujour, soon after 1800, "where there is less generosity in the souls, and in the heads fewer of those illusions which make the charm or the consolation of life. Man here weighs everything, calculates everything, and sacrifices everything to his interest." An Englishman named Fearon, in 1818, expressed the same idea with more distinctness: "In going to America, I would say generally, the emigrant must expect to find, not an economical or cleanly people; not a social or generous people; not a people of enlarged ideas; not a people of liberal opinions, or toward whom you can express your thoughts free as air; not a people friendly to the advocates of liberty in Europe; not a people who understand liberty from investigation and principle; not a people who comprehend the meaning of the words 'honor' and 'generosity.'" Such quotations might be multiplied almost without limit. Rapacity was the accepted explanation of American peculiarities; yet every traveller was troubled by inconsistencies that required explanations of a different kind. "It is not in order to hoard that the Americans are rapacious," observed Liancourt as early as 1796. The extravagance, or what economical Europeans thought extravagance, with which American women were allowed and encouraged to spend money, was as notorious in 1790 as a century later; the recklessness with which Americans often risked their money, and the liberality with which they used it, were marked even then, in comparison with the ordinary European habit. Europeans saw such contradictions, but made no attempt to reconcile them. No foreigner of that day—neither poet, painter, nor philosopher—could detect in American life anything higher than vulgarity; for it was something beyond the range of their experience, which education and culture had not framed a formula to express. Moore came to Washington, and found there no loftier inspiration than any Federalist rhymester of Dennie's school.

> "Take Christians, Mohawks, democrats and all,
> From the rude wigwam to the Congress hall,—
> From man the savage, whether slaved or free,
> To man the civilized, less tame than he:
> 'T is one dull chaos, one unfertile strife
> Betwixt half-polished and half-barbarous life;
> Where every ill the ancient world can brew
> Is mixed with every grossness of the new;

Where all corrupts, though little can entice,
And nothing's known of luxury but vice."

Moore's two small volumes of Epistles, printed in 1807, contained much more so-called poetry of the same tone,—poetry more polished and less respectable than that of Barlow and Dwight; while, as though to prove that the Old World knew what grossness was, he embalmed in his lines the slanders which the Scotch libeller Callender invented against Jefferson:—

"The weary statesman for repose hath fled
From halls of council to his negro's shed;
Where, blest, he woos some black Aspasia's grace,
And dreams of freedom in his slave's embrace."

To leave no doubt of his meaning, he explained in a footnote that his allusion was to the President of the United States; and yet even Moore, trifler and butterfly as he was, must have seen, if he would, that between the morals of politics and society in America and those then prevailing in Europe, there was no room for comparison,—there was room only for contrast.

Moore was but an echo of fashionable England in his day. He seldom affected moral sublimity; and had he in his wanderings met a race of embodied angels, he would have sung of them or to them in the slightly erotic notes which were so well received in the society he loved to frequent and flatter. His remarks upon American character betrayed more temper than truth; but even in this respect he expressed only the common feeling of Europeans, which was echoed by the Federalist society of the United States. Englishmen especially indulged in unbounded invective against the sordid character of American society, and in shaping their national policy on this contempt they carried their theory into practice with so much energy as to produce its own refutation. To their astonishment and anger, a day came when the Americans, in defiance of self-interest and in contradiction of all the qualities ascribed to them, insisted on declaring war; and readers of this narrative will be surprised at the cry of incredulity, not unmixed with terror, with which Englishmen started to their feet when they woke from their delusion on seeing what they had been taught to call the meteor flag of England, which had burned terrific at Copenhagen and Trafalgar, suddenly waver and fall on the bloody deck of the "Guerriere." Fearon and Beaujour, with a score of other contemporary critics, could see neither generosity, economy, honor, nor ideas of any kind in the American breast; yet the obstinate repetition of these denials itself betrayed a lurking fear of the social forces whose strength they were candid enough to record. What was it that, as they complained, turned the European peasant into a new man within half an hour after landing at New York? Englishmen were never at a loss to understand the poetry of more prosaic emotions. Neither they nor any of their kindred failed in later times to feel the "large excitement" of the country boy, whose "spirit leaped within him to be gone before him," when the lights of London first flared in the distance; yet none seemed ever to feel the larger excitement of the American immigrant. Among the Englishmen who criticised the United States was one greater than Moore,—one who thought himself at home only in the stern beauty of a moral presence. Of all poets, living or dead, Wordsworth felt most keenly what he called the still, sad music of humanity; yet the highest conception he could create of America was not more poetical than that of any Cumberland beggar he might have met in his morning walk:—

"Long-wished-for sight, the Western World appeared;
And when the ship was moored, I leaped ashore
Indignantly,—resolved to be a man,
Who, having o'er the past no power, would live

No longer in subjection to the past,
With abject mind—from a tyrannic lord
Inviting penance, fruitlessly endured.
So, like a fugitive whose feet have cleared
Some boundary which his followers may not cross
In prosecution of their deadly chase,
Respiring, I looked round. How bright the sun,
The breeze how soft! Can anything produced
In the Old World compare, thought I, for power
And majesty, with this tremendous stream
Sprung from the desert? And behold a city
Fresh, youthful, and aspiring!...

                          Sooth to say,

On nearer view, a motley spectacle
Appeared, of high pretensions—unreproved
But by the obstreperous voice of higher still;
Big passions strutting on a petty stage,
Which a detached spectator may regard
Not unamused. But ridicule demands
Quick change of objects; and to laugh alone,
...in the very centre of the crowd
To keep the secret of a poignant scorn,

                                ...is least fit

For the gross spirit of mankind."

Thus Wordsworth, although then at his prime, indulging in what sounded like a boast that he alone had felt the sense sublime of something interfused, whose dwelling is the light of setting suns, and the round ocean, and the living air, and the blue sky, and in the mind of man,—even he, to whose moods the heavy and the weary weight of all this unintelligible world was lightened by his deeper sympathies with nature and the soul, could do no better, when he stood in the face of American democracy, than "keep the secret of a poignant scorn."

Possibly the view of Wordsworth and Moore, of Weld, Dennie, and Dickens was right. The American democrat possessed little art of expression, and did not watch his own emotions with a view of uttering them either in prose or verse; he never told more of himself than the world might have assumed without listening to him. Only with diffidence could history attribute to such a class of men a wider range of thought or feeling than they themselves cared to proclaim. Yet the difficulty of denying or even ignoring the wider range was still greater, for no one questioned the force or the scope of an emotion which caused the poorest peasant in Europe to see what was invisible to poet and philosopher,—the dim outline of a mountain-summit across the ocean, rising high above the mist and mud of American democracy. As though to call attention to some such difficulty, European and American critics, while affirming that Americans were a race without illusions or enlarged ideas, declared in the same breath that Jefferson was a visionary whose theories would cause the heavens to fall upon them. Year after year, with endless iteration, in every accent of contempt, rage, and despair, they repeated this charge against Jefferson. Every foreigner and Federalist agreed that he was a man of illusions, dangerous to society and unbounded in power of evil; but if this view of his character was right, the same visionary qualities seemed also to be a national trait, for every one admitted that Jefferson's opinions, in one form or another, were shared by a majority of the American people.

Illustrations might be carried much further, and might be drawn from every social class and from every period in national history. Of all presidents, Abraham Lincoln has been considered the most typical representative of American society, chiefly because his mind, with all its practical qualities, also inclined, in certain directions, to idealism. Lincoln was born in 1809, the moment when American character stood in lowest esteem. Ralph Waldo Emerson, a more distinct idealist, was born in

1803. William Ellery Channing, another idealist, was born in 1780. Men like John Fitch, Oliver Evans, Robert Fulton, Joel Barlow, John Stevens, and Eli Whitney were all classed among visionaries. The whole society of Quakers belonged in the same category. The records of the popular religious sects abounded in examples of idealism and illusion to such an extent that the masses seemed hardly to find comfort or hope in any authority, however old or well established. In religion as in politics, Americans seemed to require a system which gave play to their imagination and their hopes.

Some misunderstanding must always take place when the observer is at cross-purposes with the society he describes. Wordsworth might have convinced himself by a moment's thought that no country could act on the imagination as America acted upon the instincts of the ignorant and poor, without some quality that deserved better treatment than poignant scorn; but perhaps this was only one among innumerable cases in which the unconscious poet breathed an atmosphere which the self-conscious poet could not penetrate. With equal reason he might have taken the opposite view,—that the hard, practical, money-getting American democrat, who had neither generosity nor honor nor imagination, and who inhabited cold shades where fancy sickened and where genius died, was in truth living in a world of dream, and acting a drama more instinct with poetry than all the avatars of the East, walking in gardens of emerald and rubies, in ambition already ruling the world and guiding Nature with a kinder and wiser hand than had ever yet been felt in human history. From this point his critics never approached him,—they stopped at a stone's throw; and at the moment when they declared that the man's mind had no illusions, they added that he was a knave or a lunatic. Even on his practical and sordid side, the American might easily have been represented as a victim to illusion. If the Englishman had lived as the American speculator did,—in the future,—the hyperbole of enthusiasm would have seemed less monstrous. "Look at my wealth!" cried the American to his foreign visitor. "See these solid mountains of salt and iron, of lead, copper, silver, and gold! See these magnificent cities scattered broadcast to the Pacific! See my cornfields rustling and waving in the summer breeze from ocean to ocean, so far that the sun itself is not high enough to mark where the distant mountains bound my golden seas! Look at this continent of mine, fairest of created worlds, as she lies turning up to the sun's never-failing caress her broad and exuberant breasts, overflowing with milk for her hundred million children! See how she glows with youth, health, and love!" Perhaps it was not altogether unnatural that the foreigner, on being asked to see what needed centuries to produce, should have looked about him with bewilderment and indignation. "Gold! cities! cornfields! continents! Nothing of the sort! I see nothing but tremendous wastes, where sickly men and women are dying of homesickness or are scalped by savages! mountain-ranges a thousand miles long, with no means of getting to them, and nothing in them when you get there! swamps and forests choked with their own rotten ruins! nor hope of better for a thousand years! Your story is a fraud, and you are a liar and swindler!"

Met in this spirit, the American, half perplexed and half defiant, retaliated by calling his antagonist a fool, and by mimicking his heavy tricks of manner. For himself he cared little, but his dream was his whole existence. The men who denounced him admitted that they left him in his forest-swamp quaking with fever, but clinging in the delirium of death to the illusions of his dazzled brain. No class of men could be required to support their convictions with a steadier faith, or pay more devotedly with their persons for the mistakes of their judgment. Whether imagination or greed led them to describe more than actually existed, they still saw no more than any inventor or discoverer must have seen in order to give him the energy of success. They said to the rich as to the poor, "Come and share our limitless riches! Come and help us bring to light these unimaginable stores of wealth and power!" The poor came, and from them were seldom heard complaints of deception or delusion. Within a moment, by the mere contact of a moral atmosphere, they saw the gold and jewels, the summer cornfields and the glowing continent. The rich for a long time stood aloof,— they were timid and narrow-minded; but this was not all,— between them and the American democrat was a gulf.

The charge that Americans were too fond of money to win the confidence of Europeans was a curious inconsistency; yet this was a common belief. If the American deluded himself and led others to their death by baseless speculations; if he buried those he loved in a gloomy forest where they quaked and died while he persisted in seeing there a splendid, healthy, and well-built city,—no one could deny that he sacrificed wife and child to his greed for gain, that the dollar was his god, and a sordid avarice his demon. Yet had this been the whole truth, no European capitalist would have hesitated to make money out of his grave; for, avarice against avarice, no more sordid or meaner type existed in America than could be shown on every 'Change in Europe. With much more reason Americans might have suspected that in America Englishmen found everywhere a silent influence, which they found nowhere in Europe, and which had nothing to do with avarice or with the dollar, but, on the contrary, seemed likely at any moment to sacrifice the dollar in a cause and for an object so illusory that most Englishmen could not endure to hear it discussed. European travellers who passed through America noticed that everywhere, in the White House at Washington and in log-cabins beyond the Alleghanies, except for a few Federalists, every American, from Jefferson and Gallatin down to the poorest squatter, seemed to nourish an idea that he was doing what he could to overthrow the tyranny which the past had fastened on the human mind.

Nothing was easier than to laugh at the ludicrous expressions of this simple-minded conviction, or to cry out against its coarseness, or grow angry with its prejudices; to see its nobler side, to feel the beatings of a heart underneath the sordid surface of a gross humanity, was not so easy. Europeans seemed seldom or never conscious that the sentiment could possess a noble side, but found only matter for complaint in the remark that every American democrat believed himself to be working for the overthrow of tyranny, aristocracy, hereditary privilege, and priesthood, wherever they existed. Even where the American did not openly proclaim this conviction in words, he carried so dense an atmosphere of the sentiment with him in his daily life as to give respectable Europeans an uneasy sense of remoteness.

Of all historical problems, the nature of a national character is the most difficult and the most important. Readers will be troubled, at almost every chapter of the coming narrative, by the want of some formula to explain what share the popular imagination bore in the system pursued by government. The acts of the American people during the administrations of Jefferson and Madison were judged at the time by no other test. According as bystanders believed American character to be hard, sordid, and free from illusion, they were severe and even harsh in judgment. This rule guided the governments of England and France. Federalists in the United States, knowing more of the circumstances, often attributed to the democratic instinct a visionary quality which they regarded as sentimentality, and charged with many bad consequences. If their view was correct, history could occupy itself to no better purpose than in ascertaining the nature and force of the quality which was charged with results so serious; but nothing was more elusive than the spirit of American democracy. Jefferson, the literary representative of the class, spoke chiefly for Virginians, and dreaded so greatly his own reputation as a visionary that he seldom or never uttered his whole thought. Gallatin and Madison were still more cautious. The press in no country could give shape to a mental condition so shadowy. The people themselves, although millions in number, could not have expressed their finer instincts had they tried, and might not have recognized them if expressed by others.

In the early days of colonization, every new settlement represented an idea and proclaimed a mission. Virginia was founded by a great, liberal movement aiming at the spread of English liberty and empire. The Pilgrims of Plymouth, the Puritans of Boston, the Quakers of Pennsylvania, all avowed a moral purpose, and began by making institutions that consciously reflected a moral idea. No such character belonged to the colonization of 1800. From Lake Erie to Florida, in long, unbroken line, pioneers were at work, cutting into the forests with the energy of so many beavers, and with no more express moral purpose than the beavers they drove away. The civilization they carried with them was rarely illumined by an idea; they sought room for no new truth, and aimed neither at creating, like the Puritans, a government of saints, nor, like the Quakers, one of love and peace; they left such experiments behind them, and wrestled only with the hardest problems of frontier life. No wonder that foreign observers, and even the educated, well-to-do Americans of the sea-coast, could seldom see anything to admire in the ignorance and brutality of frontiersmen, and should declare that virtue and wisdom no longer guided the United States! What they saw was not encouraging. To a new society, ignorant and semi-barbarous, a mass of demagogues insisted on applying every stimulant that could inflame its worst appetites, while at the same instant taking away every influence that had hitherto helped to restrain its passions. Greed for wealth, lust for power, yearning for the blank void of savage freedom such as Indians and wolves delighted in,—these were the fires that flamed under the caldron of American society, in which, as conservatives believed, the old, well-proven, conservative crust of religion, government, family, and even common respect for age, education, and experience was rapidly melting away, and was indeed already broken into fragments, swept about by the seething mass of scum ever rising in greater quantities to the surface.

Against this Federalist and conservative view of democratic tendencies, democrats protested in a thousand forms, but never in any mode of expression which satisfied them all, or explained their whole character. Probably Jefferson came nearest to the mark, for he represented the hopes of science as well as the prejudices of Virginia; but Jefferson's writings may be searched from beginning to end without revealing the whole measure of the man, far less of the movement. Here and there in his letters a suggestion was thrown out, as though by chance, revealing larger hopes,—as in 1815, at a moment of despondency, he wrote: "I fear from the experience of the last twenty-five years that morals do not of necessity advance hand in hand with the sciences." In 1800, in the flush of triumph, he believed that his task in the world was to establish a democratic republic, with the sciences for an intellectual field, and physical and moral advancement keeping pace with their advance. Without an excessive introduction of more recent ideas, he might be imagined to define democratic progress, in the somewhat affected precision of his French philosophy: "Progress is either physical or intellectual. If we can bring it about that men are on the average an inch taller in the next generation than in this; if they are an inch larger round the chest; if their brain is an ounce or two heavier, and their life a year or two longer,—that is progress. If fifty years hence the average man shall invariably argue from two ascertained premises where he now jumps to a conclusion from a single supposed revelation,—that is progress! I expect it to be made here, under our democratic stimulants, on a great scale, until every man is potentially an athlete in body and an Aristotle in mind." To this doctrine the New Englander replied, "What will you do for moral progress?" Every possible answer to this question opened a chasm. No doubt Jefferson held the faith that men would improve morally with their physical and intellectual growth; but he had no idea of any moral improvement other than that which came by nature. He could not tolerate a priesthood, a state church, or revealed religion. Conservatives, who could tolerate no society without such pillars of order, were, from their point of view, right in answering, "Give us rather the worst despotism of Europe,— there our souls at least may have a chance of salvation!" To their minds vice and virtue were not relative, but fixed terms. The Church was a divine institution. How could a ship hope to reach port when the crew threw overboard sails, spars, and compass, unshipped their rudder, and all the long day thought only of eating and drinking. Nay, even should the new experiment succeed in a worldly sense, what was a man profited if he gained the whole world, and lost his own soul? The Lord God was a jealous God, and visited the sins of the parents upon the children; but what worse sin could be conceived than for a whole nation to join their chief in chanting the strange hymn with which Jefferson, a new false prophet, was deceiving and betraying his people: "It does me no injury for my neighbor to say there are twenty Gods or no God!"

On this ground conservatism took its stand, as it had hitherto done with success in every similar emergency in the world's history, and fixing its eyes on moral standards of its own, refused to deal with the subject as further open to argument. The two parties stood facing opposite ways, and could see no common ground of contact.

Yet even then one part of the American social system was proving itself to be rich in results. The average American was more intelligent than the average European, and was becoming every year still more active-minded as the new movement of society caught him up and swept him through a life of more varied experiences. On all sides the national mind responded to its stimulants. Deficient as the American was in the machinery of higher instruction; remote, poor; unable by any exertion to acquire the training, the capital, or even the elementary text-books he needed for a fair development of his natural pow-ers,—his native energy and ambition already responded to the spur applied to them. Some of his triumphs were famous throughout the world; for Benjamin Franklin had raised high the reputation of American printers, and the actual President of the United States, who signed with Franklin the treaty of peace with Great Britain, was the son of a small farmer, and had him-self kept a school in his youth. In both these cases social recog-nition followed success; but the later triumphs of the American mind were becoming more and more popular. John Fitch was not only one of the poorest, but one of the least-educated Yankees who ever made a name; he could never spell with toler-able correctness, and his life ended as it began,—in the lowest social obscurity. Eli Whitney was better educated than Fitch, but had neither wealth, social influence, nor patron to back his ingenuity. In the year 1800 Eli Terry, another Connecticut Yankee of the same class, took into his employ two young men to help him make wooden clocks, and this was the capital on which the greatest clock-manufactory in the world began its operations. In 1797 Asa Whittemore, a Massachusetts Yankee, invented a machine to make cards for carding wool, which "op-erated as if it had a soul," and became the foundation for a hundred subsequent patents. In 1790 Jacob Perkins, of New-buryport, invented a machine capable of cutting and turning out two hundred thousand nails a day; and then invented a process for transferring engraving from a very small steel cylin-der to copper, which revolutionized cotton-printing. The Brit-ish traveller Weld, passing through Wilmington, stopped, as Liancourt had done before him, to see the great flour-mills on the Brandywine. "The improvements," he said, "which have been made in the machinery of the flour-mills in America are very great. The chief of these consist in a new application of the screw, and the introduction of what are called elevators, the idea of which was evidently borrowed from the chain-pump." This was the invention of Oliver Evans, a native of Delaware, whose parents were in very humble life, but who was himself, in spite of every disadvantage, an inventive genius of the first order. Robert Fulton, who in 1800 was in Paris with Joel Barlow, sprang from the same source in Pennsylvania. John Stevens, a native of New York, belonged to a more favored class, but followed the same impulses. All these men were the outcome of typical American society, and all their inventions transmuted the democratic instinct into a practical and tangible shape. Who would undertake to say that there was a limit to the fecundity of this teeming source? Who that saw only the narrow, practical, money-getting nature of these devices could venture to assert that as they wrought their end and raised the standard of millions, they would not also raise the creative power of those millions to a higher plane? If the priests and barons who set their names to Magna Charta had been told that in a few centuries every swine-herd and cobbler's apprentice would write and read with an ease such as few kings could then command, and reason with better logic than any university could then practise, the priest and baron would have been more incredulous than any man who was told in 1800 that within another five centuries the ploughboy would go a-field whistling a sonata of Beethoven, and figure out in quaternions the relation of his furrows. The American democrat knew so little of art that among his popular illusions he could not then nourish artistic ambition; but leaders like Jefferson, Gallatin, and Barlow might without extravagance count upon a coming time when diffused ease and education should bring the masses into familiar contact with higher forms of human achievement, and their vast creative power, turned toward a nobler culture, might rise to the level of that democratic genius which found expression in the Parthenon; might revel in the delights of a new Buonarotti and a richer Titian; might create for five hundred million people the America of thought and art which alone could satisfy their omnivorous ambition.

Whether the illusions, so often affirmed and so often denied to the American people, took such forms or not, these were in effect the problems that lay before American society: Could it transmute its social power into the higher forms of thought? Could it provide for the moral and intellectual needs of mankind? Could it take permanent political shape? Could it give new life to religion and art? Could it create and maintain in the mass of mankind those habits of mind which had hitherto belonged to men of science alone? Could it physically develop the convolutions of the human brain? Could it produce, or was it compatible with, the differentiation of a higher variety of the human race? Nothing less than this was necessary for its complete success.

PART TWO

America in 1817

Economical Results

THE UNION, which contained 5,300,000 inhabitants in 1800, numbered 7,240,000 in 1810, and 9,634,000 in 1820. At the close of Madison's Administration, in 1817, the population probably numbered not less than 8,750,000 persons. The average rate of annual increase was about three and five-tenths per cent, causing the population to double within twenty-three years.

The rate of increase was not uniform throughout the country, but the drift of population was well defined. In 1800 the five New England States contained about 1,240,000 persons. Virginia and North Carolina, united, then contained nearly 1,360,000, or ten per cent more than New England. In 1820 the two groups were still nearer equality. New England numbered about 1,665,000; the two Southern States numbered 1,700,000, or about two per cent more than New England. While these two groups, containing nearly half the population of the Union, increased only as one hundred to one hundred and twenty-nine, the middle group, comprising New York, New Jersey, and Pennsylvania, increased in the relation of one hundred to one hundred and ninety-two,—from 1,402,000 in 1800, to 2,696,000 in 1820. Their rate was about the average ratio for the Union; and the three Western States,—Ohio, Kentucky, and Tennessee,—grew proportionally faster. Their population of 370,000 in 1800 became 1,567,000 in 1820, in the ratio of one hundred to four hundred and twenty-three.

Careful study revealed a situation alarming to New England and Virginia. If only Connecticut, Rhode Island, and Massachusetts, without its district of Maine, were considered, a total population numbering 742,000 in 1800 increased only to 881,000 in 1820, or in the ratio of one hundred to one hundred and eighteen in twenty years. If only the white population of Virginia and North Carolina were taken into the estimate, omitting the negroes, 852,000 persons in 1800 increased to 1,022,000 in 1820, or in the ratio of one hundred to one hundred and twenty. Maryland showed much the same result, while Delaware, which rose from 64,270 in 1800 to 72,674 in 1810, remained stationary, numbering only 72,749 in 1820,—a gain of seventy-five persons in ten years. The white population showed a positive decrease, from 55,361 in 1810 to 55,282 in 1820.

Probably a census taken in 1817 would have given results still less favorable to the sea-coast. The war affected population more seriously than could have been reasonably expected, and stopped the growth of the large cities. New York in 1800 contained 60,000 persons; in 1810 it contained 96,400, but a corporation census of 1816 reported a population of only one hundred thousand, although two of the six years were years of peace and prosperity. From that time New York grew rapidly, numbering 124,000 in 1820,—a gain of about twenty-five per cent in four years. Even the interior town of Albany, which should have been stimulated by the war, and which increased four thousand in population between 1800 and 1810, increased only three thousand between 1810 and 1820. Philadelphia fared worse, for its population of 96,000 in 1810 grew only to 108,000 in 1820, and fell rapidly behind New York. Baltimore grew from 26,000 in 1800 to 46,000 in 1810, and numbered less than 63,000 in 1820. Boston suffered more than Baltimore; for its population, which numbered 24,000 in 1800, grew only to 32,000 in 1810, and numbered but 43,000 in 1820. Charleston was still more unfortunate. In 1800 its population numbered about eighteen thousand; in 1810, 24,700; in 1817 a local census reported a decrease to 23,950 inhabitants, and the national census of 1820 reported 24,780, or eighty persons more than in 1810. The town of Charleston and the State of Delaware increased together by the same numbers.

Although the war lasted less than three years, its effect was so great in checking the growth of the cities that during the period from 1810 to 1820 the urban population made no relative increase. During every other decennial period in the national history the city population grew more rapidly than that of the rural districts; but between 1810 and 1820 it remained stationary, at four and nine-tenths per cent of the entire population. While Boston, Philadelphia, and Charleston advanced slowly, and New York only doubled its population in twenty years, Western towns like Pittsburg, Cincinnati, and Louisville grew rapidly and steadily, and even New Orleans, though exposed to capture, more than trebled in size; but the Western towns were still too small to rank as important. Even in 1820 the only cities which contained a white population of more than twenty thousand were New York, Philadelphia, Baltimore, and Boston.

The severest sufferers from this situation were the three southern States of New England,—Connecticut, Rhode Island, and Massachusetts, excluding the district of Maine, which was about to become a separate State. Fortunately the northern part of New England, notwithstanding the war, increased much more rapidly than the southern portion; but this increase was chiefly at the cost of Massachusetts, and returned little in comparison with the loss. The situation of Massachusetts and Connecticut was dark. Had not wealth increased more rapidly than population, Massachusetts would have stood on the verge of ruin; yet even from the economical point of view, the outlook was not wholly cheerful.

Judged by the reports of Massachusetts banks, the increase of wealth was surprising. The official returns of 1803, the first year when such returns were made, reported seven banks in the State, with a capital of $2,225,000 and deposits of $1,500,000. In June, 1816, twenty-five banks returned capital stock amounting nearly to $11,500,000 and deposits of $2,133,000. The deposits were then small, owing to the decline of industry and drain of specie that followed the peace, but the capital invested in banks had more than quintupled in thirteen years.

This multiplication was not a correct measure of the general increase in wealth. Indeed, the banks were in excess of the public wants after the peace, and their capital quickly shrunk from $11,500,000 in June, 1816, to $9,300,000 in June, 1817, a decline of nearly twenty per cent in a year. From that time it began to increase again, and held its improvement even in the disastrous year 1819. Assuming 1803 and 1817 as the true terms of the equation, the banking capital of Massachusetts increased in fourteen years from $2,225,000 to $9,300,000, or more than quadrupled.

Gauged by bank discounts the increase of wealth was not so great. In 1803 the debts due to the banks were returned at $3,850,000; in June, 1817, they were $12,650,000. If the discounts showed the true growth of industry, the business of the State somewhat more than trebled in fourteen years. Probably the chief industries that used the increased banking capital were the new manufactures, for the older sources of Massachusetts wealth showed no equivalent gain. Tested by the imports, the improvement was moderate. In 1800 the gross amount of duties collected in Massachusetts was less than $3,200,000; in 1816 it somewhat exceeded $6,100,000, but had not permanently doubled in sixteen years. Tested by exports of domestic produce, Massachusetts showed no gain. In 1803 the value of such produce amounted to $5,400,000; in 1816, to $5,008,000.

Other methods of calculating the increase of wealth gave equally contradictory results. The registered tonnage of Massachusetts engaged in foreign trade exceeded two hundred and ten thousand tons in 1800; in 1816 it was two hundred and seventy-four thousand tons. In the coasting-trade Massachusetts employed seventy-five thousand tons in 1800, and one hundred and twenty-nine thousand in 1816. The tonnage employed in the fisheries showed no growth. The shipping of Massachusetts seemed to indicate an increase of about forty per cent in sixteen years.

The system of direct taxation furnished another standard of comparison. In 1798 a valuation was made in certain States of houses and lands for direct taxes; another was made in 1813; a third in 1815. That of 1798 amounted to eighty-four million dollars for Massachusetts; that of 1813, to one hundred and forty-nine millions; that of 1815, to one hundred and forty-three millions,—a gain of seventy per cent in sixteen years; but such a valuation in 1817 would probably have shown a considerable loss on that of 1815.

Evidently the chief increase in wealth consisted in the growth of manufactures, but after the prostration of the manufacturing interest in 1816 no plausible estimate of their true value could be made, unless the bank discounts measured their progress. The result of the whole inquiry, though vague, suggested that wealth had increased in Massachusetts more rapidly than population, and had possibly gained seventy or eighty per cent in sixteen years; but in spite of this increase the State was in a pitiable situation. Neither steamboats, canals, nor roads could help it. Thousands of its citizens migrated to New York and Ohio, beyond the possibility of future advantage to the land they left. Manufactures were prostrate. Shipping was driven from the carrying trade. Taxation weighed far more heavily than ever before. A load of obloquy rested on the State on account of its war policy and the Hartford Convention. The national government treated it with severity, and refused to pay for the Massachusetts militia called into service by the

President during the war, because the governor had refused to place them under national officers.

The condition of Massachusetts and Maine was a picture of New England. Democratic Rhode Island suffered equally with Federalist Connecticut. Maine, New Hampshire, and Vermont showed growth, but the chief possibility of replacing lost strength lay in immigration. During the European wars, no considerable number of immigrants were able to reach the United States; but immediately after the return of peace, emigration from Europe to America began on a scale as alarming to European governments as the movement to western New York and Ohio was alarming to the seaboard States of the Union. During the year 1817 twenty-two thousand immigrants were reported as entering the United States. Twelve or fourteen thousand were probably Irish; four thousand were German. More than two thousand arrived in Boston, while about seven thousand landed in New York and the same number in Philadelphia. The greater part probably remained near where they landed, and in some degree supplied the loss of natives who went west. The rapid growth of the northern cities of the seacoast began again only with the flood of immigration.

Although the three southern States of New England were the severest sufferers, the Virginia group—comprising Delaware, Maryland, Virginia, and North Carolina—escaped little better. In twenty years their white population increased nineteen and five tenths per cent, while that of Massachusetts, Connecticut, and Rhode Island increased eighteen per cent. The wealth of Southern States consisted largely in slaves; and the negro population of the Virginia group increased about twenty-five per cent in numbers during the sixteen years from 1800 to 1816. The exports of domestic produce increased about forty per cent in value, comparing the average of 1801–1805 with that of 1815–1816. The net revenue collected in Virginia increased nearly seventy per cent, comparing the year 1815 with the average of the five years 1800–1804; while that collected in North Carolina more than doubled.

Measured by these standards, the growth of wealth in the Virginia group of States was not less rapid than in Massachusetts, and the same conclusion was established by other methods. In 1816 Virginia contained two State banks, with branches, which returned for January 1 a capital stock of $4,590,000, with a note circulation of $6,000,000, and deposits approaching $2,500,000. Their discounts amounted to $7,768,000 in January, 1816, and were contracted to $6,128,000 in the following month of November. Although Virginia used only half the banking capital and credits required by Massachusetts, the rate of increase was equally rapid, and the tendency toward banking was decided. In 1817 the legislature created two new banks, one for the valley of Virginia, the other for western Virginia, with a capital stock of $600,000, and branches with capital stock of $100,000 for each. Between 1800 and 1817, banking capital exceeding five million dollars was created in Virginia, where none had existed before.

If the estimates made by Timothy Pitkin, the best statistician of the time, were correct, the returns for direct taxes showed a greater increase of wealth in Virginia than in Massachusetts. The valuation of Virginia for 1799 was $71,000,000; that of 1815 was $165,000,000. The valuation of North Carolina in 1799 was $30,000,000; that of 1815 was $51,000,000. Maryland was estimated at $32,000,000 in 1799, at $106,000,000 in 1815. The average increase for the three States was in the ratio of one hundred to two hundred and forty, while that for Massachusetts, Rhode Island, and Connecticut was nearer one hundred to one hundred and seventy-five. The normal increase for the Union was in the ratio of one hundred to two hundred and sixty-three.

The result obtained from the estimates for direct taxes was affected by a doubt in regard to the correctness of the valuation of 1799, which was believed to have been too low in the Southern States; but the general conclusion could not be doubted that the Virginia group of States increased steadily in wealth. The rapidity of increase was concealed by an equally rapid impoverishment of the old tobacco-planting aristocracy, whose complaints drowned argument. As the lands of the ancient families became exhausted, the families themselves fell into poverty, or emigrated to the richer Ohio valley. Their decline or departure gave rise to many regrets and alarms. With the impressions thus created, the people associated the want of economical machinery as a cause of their backwardness, and became clamorous for roads, canals, and banks. The revolution in their ideas between 1800 and 1816 was complete.

The North Carolinians were first to denounce their old habits of indifference, and to declare their State in danger of ruin on that account. A committee of the State legislature reported Nov. 30, 1815, that vigorous measures for self-protection could no longer be postponed:—

> "With an extent of territory sufficient to maintain more than ten millions of inhabitants, . . . we can only boast of a population something less than six hundred thousand, and it is but too obvious that this population under the present state of things already approaches its maximum. Within twenty-five years past more than two hundred thousand of our inhabitants have removed to the waters of the Ohio, Tennessee, and Mobile; and it is mortifying to witness the fact that thousands of our wealthy and respectable citizens are annually moving to the West, . . . and that thousands of our poorer citizens follow them, being literally driven away by the prospect of poverty. In this state of things our agriculture is at a stand."

The Virginians showed an equally strong sense of their perils. Twelve months after the North Carolina legislature took the matter in hand, a committee of the Virginia legislature in December, 1816, discussed the same topic and reached the same conclusion. Although something had been done by corporations to open canals on the Potomac, the James River, and to the Dismal Swamp, the State of Virginia had in sixteen years made little advance in material welfare. While New England had built turnpikes wherever a profit could be expected, in Virginia, said the committee, "the turnpike-roads of the Commonwealth, except a few short passes of particular mountains and a road recently begun from Fredericksburg to the Blue Ridge, are confined principally to the county of Loudon, the adjacent counties of Fairfax, Fauquier, and Frederick, and to the vicinity of the seat of government." In other respects the situation was worse.

"While many other States," said the committee, "have been advancing in wealth and numbers with a rapidity which has astonished themselves, the ancient Dominion and elder sister of the Union has remained stationary. A very large proportion of her western territory is yet unimproved, while a considerable part of her eastern has receded from its former opulence. How many sad spectacles do her low-lands present of wasted and deserted fields, of dwellings abandoned by their proprietors, of churches in ruins! The genius of her ancient hospitality, benumbed by the cold touch of penury, spreads his scanty hoard in naked halls, or seeks a coarser but more plenteous repast in the lonely cabins of the West. The fathers of the land are gone where another outlet to the ocean turns their thoughts from the place of their nativity, and their affections from the haunts of their youth."

Another committee reported to the House of Delegates Jan. 5, 1816, in favor of extending the banking system of the State. The report used language new as an expression of Virginian opinions.

"Your committee believe that a prejudice has gone abroad, which they confidently trust experience will prove to be unfounded even to the satisfaction of those by whom it is entertained, that the policy of Virginia is essentially hostile to commerce and to the rights of commercial men. Upon the removal of this prejudice must depend the future contributions of this Commonwealth toward the prosperity and glory if not the happiness and safety of the United States. Without the confidence of foreigners there can exist no foreign commerce. Without foreign commerce there can exist neither ships, seamen, nor a navy; and a tremendous lesson has taught Virginia that without a navy she can have no security for her repose."

Notwithstanding the gloom of these recitals, the evidence tended to show that while the white population of Virginia increased only about nineteen per cent in sixteen years, its wealth nearly doubled. Comparison with the quicker growth of the Middle States—New York, New Jersey, and Pennsylvania—caused much of the uneasiness felt by New England and Virginia. The banking capital of New York, which probably did not much exceed three million dollars in 1800, amounted in 1816 to nearly $19,000,000; that of Pennsylvania exceeded $16,000,000. The valuation of houses and lands for the direct tax rose in New York from $100,000,000 in 1799 to nearly $270,000,000 in 1815; and in Pennsylvania, from $102,000,000 in 1799 to $346,000,000 in 1815. The net revenue collected in New York was $2,700,000 in 1800, and $14,500,000 in 1815; that collected in Pennsylvania was $1,350,000 in 1800, and

$7,140,000 in 1815. This rate of increase did not extend to exports. The value of the domestic exports from New York in 1803 was about $7,500,000; in 1816 it exceeded $14,000,000; while the value of Pennsylvanian exports increased little,—being $4,021,000 in 1803 and $4,486,000 in 1816. The population of New York doubled while that of Massachusetts and Virginia hardly increased one third. Pennsylvania grew less rapidly in numbers, but still about twice as fast as New England.

Although this rate of progress seemed to leave New England and Virginia far behind the Middle States, it was less striking than the other economical changes already accomplished or foreseen. The movement of population or of wealth was not so important as the methods by which the movement was effected. The invention of the steamboat gave a decisive advantage to New York over every rival. Already in 1816 the system had united New York city so closely with distant places that a traveller could go from New York to Philadelphia by steamboat and stage in thirteen hours; or to Albany in twenty-four hours; and taking stage to Whitehall in twelve hours could reach Montreal in thirty hours, and go on to Quebec in twenty-four hours,—thus consuming about five and a half successive days in the long journey from Philadelphia to Quebec, sleeping comfortably on his way, and all at an expense of fifty dollars. This economy of time and money was a miracle; but New York could already foresee that it led to other advantages of immeasurable value. The steamboat gave impetus to travel, and was a blessing to travellers; but its solid gain for the prosperity of the United States lay not in passenger traffic so much as in freight, and New York was the natural centre of both.

While Pennsylvania, Virginia, and the Carolinas were building roads and canals across a hundred miles of mountains, only to reach at last an interior region which enjoyed an easier outlet for freight, New York had but to people a level and fertile district, nowhere fifty miles from navigable water, in order to reach the great Lake system, which had no natural outlet within the Union except through the city of New York. So obvious was the idea of a canal from the Lakes to the Hudson that it was never out of men's minds, even before the war; and no sooner did peace return than the scheme took large proportions. Active leaders of both political parties pressed the plan, —De Witt Clinton, Gouverneur Morris, and Peter B. Porter were all concerned in it; but the legislature and people then supposed that so vast an undertaking as a canal to connect Lake Erie with the ocean, national in character and military in its probable utility, required national aid. Supposing the Administration to be pledged to the policy outlined by Gallatin and approved by Jefferson in the Annual Message of 1806, the New York commissioners applied to Congress for assistance, and uniting with other local interests procured the passage of Calhoun's bill for internal improvements.

They were met by Madison's veto. This act, although at first it seemed to affect most the interests of New York, was in reality injurious only to the Southern States. Had the government lent its aid to the Erie Canal, it must have assisted similar schemes elsewhere, and in the end could hardly have refused to carry out Gallatin's plan of constructing canals from the Chesapeake to the Ohio, and from the Santee to the Tennessee River. The veto disappointed New York only for the moment, but was fatal to Southern hopes. After the first shock of discouragement, the New York legislature determined to persevere, and began the work without assistance. The legislature of Pennsylvania at the same time appropriated half a million dollars for roads and canals, and for improvements of river navigation, devoting nearly one hundred and fifty thousand dollars to aid the turnpike-road to Pittsburg. The fund established by the State of Ohio, as a condition of its admission to the Union, had in 1816 produced means to construct the National or Cumberland Road to the hundred and thirteenth mile. The indifference to internal improvements which had been so marked a popular trait in 1800, gave place to universal interest and activity in 1816; but the Middle States were far in advance of the Eastern and Southern in opening communications with the West; and New York, owing in no small degree to the veto, could already foresee the time when it would wrest from Pennsylvania the supply of the valley of the Ohio, while expanding new tributary territory to an indefinite extent along the Lakes.

When Madison retired from the Presidency, the limits of civilization, though rapidly advancing, were still marked by the Indian boundary, which extended from the western end of Lake Erie across Indiana, Kentucky, Tennessee, and the South-western territory. Only weak and helpless tribes remained east of the Mississippi, waiting until the whites should require the surrender of their lands; but the whites, already occupying land far in advance of their needs, could not yet take the whole. Not until 1826 were the Indian titles generally extinguished throughout Indiana. The military work was done, and the short space of sixteen years had practically accomplished the settlement of the whole country as far as the Mississippi; but another generation was needed in order to take what these sixteen years had won.

As population spread, the postal service struggled after it. Except on the Hudson River, steamboats were still irregular in their trips; and for this reason the mails continued to be carried on horseback through the interior. In 1801 the number of post-offices was 957; in 1817 it was 3,459. In 1801 the length of post-roads was less than 25,000 miles; in 1817 it was 52,689. In 1800 the gross receipts from postage were $280,000; in 1817 they slightly exceeded $1,000,000. In each case the increase much surpassed the ratio for population, and offered another means for forming some estimate of the increase of wealth. The Four-teenth Congress pressed the extension of post-routes in western New York, Ohio, and Indiana; they were already established beyond the Mississippi. Rapidity of motion was also increased on the main routes. From New York to Buffalo, four hundred and seventy-five miles, the traveller went at an average rate of five miles an hour, and, sleeping every night, he arrived in about four days. Between Philadelphia and Pittsburg, where no watercourse shortened the distance, the stage-coach consumed five and a half days, allowing for stoppage at night. These rates of travel were equal to those common on routes of similar length in Europe; but long after 1817 the mail from Washington to New Orleans, by a route 1,380 miles in length, required twenty-four days of travel.

Had the steamboat system been at once perfected, the mail could have been carried with much more rapidity; but the progress of the new invention was slow. After the trial trip of the "Clermont," Aug. 17, 1807, five years elapsed before the declaration of war; yet in 1812 New York possessed no other steam-line than the Albany packets. Steam-ferries plied to Hoboken, Amboy, and other places in the immediate neighborhood; but neither Newport, New London, nor New Haven enjoyed steam communication with New York until after the war. In the spring of 1813 eight or nine steamboats belonged to the city of New York, but only three, which ran to Albany, were more than ferries. At the same time Philadelphia possessed six such ferry-boats. From Baltimore a steamer ran to the head of Chesapeake Bay; but the southern coast and the town of Charleston saw no steamboat until a year after the war was ended.

The West was more favored. In 1811 a boat of four hundred tons was built at Pittsburg and sent down the river to New Orleans, where it plied between New Orleans and Natchez. Two more were built at the same place in 1813–1814; and one of them, the "Vesuvius," went down the river in the spring of 1814, rousing general interest in the midst of war by making the trip in nine days and a half, or two hundred and twenty-seven hours. The "Vesuvius" remained on the Mississippi for the next two years, but was burned with her cargo in the summer of 1816. By that time the world was thinking much of steamboats, and their use was rapidly extending, though regular trips were still uncommon except in the east.

The result of the sixteen years, considered only in the economical development of the Union, was decisive. Although population increased more rapidly than was usual in human experience, wealth accumulated still faster. From such statistics as the times afforded, a strong probability has been shown that while population doubled within twenty-three years, wealth doubled within twenty. Statistics covering the later period of national growth, warrant the belief that a valuation of $1,742,000,000 in 1800 corresponded to a valuation of $3,734,000,000 in 1820; and that if a valuation of $328 per capita is assumed for 1800, a valuation of $386 per capita may be estimated for 1820.

These sixteen years set at rest the natural doubts that had attended the nation's birth. The rate of increase both in population and wealth was established and permanent, unless indeed it should become even more rapid. Every serious difficulty which seemed alarming to the people of the Union in 1800 had been removed or had sunk from notice in 1816. With the disappearance of every immediate peril, foreign or domestic, society could devote all its energies, intellectual and physical, to its favorite objects. This result was not the only or even the chief proof that economical progress was to be at least as rapid in the future as at the time when the nation had to struggle with political difficulties. Not only had the people during these sixteen years escaped from dangers, they had also found the means of supplying their chief needs. Besides clearing away every obstacle to the occupation and development of their continent as far as the Mississippi River, they created the steamboat, the most efficient instrument yet conceived for developing such a country. The continent lay before them, like an uncovered ore-bed.

They could see, and they could even calculate with reasonable accuracy, the wealth it could be made to yield. With almost the certainty of a mathematical formula, knowing the rate of increase of population and of wealth, they could read in advance their economical history for at least a hundred years.

Religious and Political Thought

THE MOVEMENT of thought, more interesting than the movement of population or of wealth, was equally well defined. In the midst of political dissension and economical struggles, religion still took precedence; and the religious movement claimed notice not merely for its depth or for its universality, but also and especially for its direction. Religious interest and even excitement were seen almost everywhere, both in the older and in the newer parts of the country; and every such movement offered some means of studying or illustrating the development of national character. For the most part the tendency seemed emotional rather than intellectual; but in New England the old intellectual pre-eminence, which once marked the Congregational clergy, developed a quality both new and distinctive.

The Congregational clergy, battling with the innate vices of human nature, thought themselves obliged to press on their hearers the consequences of God's infinite wrath rather than those of his infinite love. They admitted that in a worldly sense they erred, and they did not deny that their preaching sometimes leaned to severity; but they would have been false to their charge and undeserving of their high character had they lost sight of their radical doctrine that every man was by nature personally depraved, and unless born again could not hope to see the kingdom of God. Many intellectual efforts had been made by many ages of men to escape the logic of this doctrine, but without success. The dogma and its consequences could not be abandoned without abandoning the Church.

From this painful dilemma a group of young Boston clergymen made a new attempt to find a path of escape. Their movement drew its inspiration from Harvard College, and was simultaneous with the sway of Jefferson's political ideas; but the relationship which existed between religious and political innovation was remote and wholly intellectual. Harvard College seemed to entertain no feeling toward Jefferson but antipathy, when in 1805 the corporation appointed Henry Ware, whose Unitarian tendencies were well known, to be Hollis Professor of Theology. The Unitarianism of Henry Ware and his supporters implied at that time no well-defined idea beyond a qualified rejection of the Trinity, and a suggestion of what they thought a more comprehensible view of Christ's divine character; but it still subverted an essential dogma of the Church, and opened the way to heresy. The Calvinists could no longer regard Harvard College as a school proper for the training of clergy; and they were obliged to establish a new theological seminary, which they attached to a previously existing Academy at Andover, in Essex County, Massachusetts. The two branches of the New England Calvinists—known then as old Calvinism and Hopkinsianism—united in framing for the instructors of the Andover school a creed on the general foundation of the Westminster Assembly's Shorter Catechism, and thus provided for the future education of their clergy in express opposition to Unitarians and Universalists.

Thenceforward the theological school of Harvard College became more and more Unitarian. The Massachusetts parishes, divided between the two schools of theology, selected, as pleased a majority of their church-members, either Orthodox or Unitarian pastors; and while the larger number remained Calvinistic, though commonly preferring ministers who avoided controversy, the Boston parishes followed the Unitarian movement, and gradually filled their pulpits with young men. The Unitarian clergy soon won for themselves and for their city a name beyond proportion with their numbers.

Joseph Stevens Buckminster, the first, and while he lived the most influential, of these preachers, began his career in 1805 by accepting a call from one of the old Boston churches. He died in 1812 at the close of his twenty-eighth year. His influence was rather social and literary than theological or controversial. During his lifetime the Unitarian movement took no definite shape, except as a centre of revived interest in all that was then supposed to be best and purest in religious, literary, and artistic feeling. After his death, Unitarians learned to regard William Ellery Channing as their most promising leader. Channing had accepted the charge of a Boston church as early as 1803, and was about four years older than Buckminster. A third active member of the Boston clergy was Samuel Cooper Thacher, who took charge of a Boston parish in 1811, and was five years younger than Channing. In all, some seven or eight churches were then called Unitarian; but they professed no uniform creed, and probably no two clergymen or parishes agreed in their understanding of the precise difference between them and the Orthodox church. Shades of difference distinguished each Unitarian parish from every other, and the degree of their divergence from the old creed was a subject of constant interest and private discussion, although the whole body of churches, Congregational as well as Unitarian, remained in external repose.

The calm was not broken until the close of the war relieved New England from a political anxiety which for fifteen years had restrained internal dissensions. No sooner did peace restore to New England the natural course of its intellectual movement than the inevitable schism broke out. In June, 1815, the "Panoplist," the mouthpiece of the Congregational clergy, published an article charging the Unitarians with pursuing an unavowed propaganda, and calling upon the Church to refuse them communion. Channing and his friends thought the attack to require reply, and, after consultation, Channing published a "Letter to the Rev. Samuel C. Thacher," which began a discussion and a theological movement of no slight interest to American history.

Channing's theology at that time claimed no merit for originality. His letter to Thacher betrayed more temper than he would afterward have shown; but in no particular was he more earnest than in repelling the idea that he or his brethren were innovators. In whatever points they disagreed, they were most nearly unanimous in repudiating connection with the English Unitarians who denied the divinity of Christ. Channing declared "that a majority of our brethren believe that Jesus Christ is more than man; that he existed before the world; that he literally came from heaven to save our race; that he sustains other offices than those of a teacher and witness to the truth; and that he still acts for our benefit, and is our intercessor with the Father." So far was Channing from wishing to preach a new theology that he would gladly have accepted the old had he thought it intelligible:

> "It is from deep conviction that I have stated once and again that the differences between Unitarians and Trinitarians lie more in sounds than in ideas; that a barbarous phraseology is the chief wall of partition between these classes of Christians; and that could Trinitarians tell us what they mean, their system would generally be found little else than a mystical form of the Unitarian doctrine."

Calvinists could not be blamed for thinking that their venerable creed, the painful outcome of the closest and most strenuous reasoning known in the Christian world, was entitled to more respect than to be called "little else than a mystical form of the Unitarian doctrine." The Unitarians themselves scarcely attempted to make the infinite more intelligible to the finite by any new phraseology. They avowed a dislike for dogma as their merit. During these early years they systematically avoided controversy; in the pulpit they never assailed and seldom mentioned other forms of Christian faith, or even the scheme of Trinity which caused their schism.

> "So deeply are we convinced," said Channing's letter, "that the great end of preaching is to promote a spirit of love, a sober, righteous, and godly life, and that every doctrine is to be urged simply and exclusively for this end, that we have sacrificed our ease, and have chosen to be less striking preachers rather than to enter the lists of controversy."

Yet the popular dislike of Calvinistic severity could not wholly make good the want of doctrinal theology. The Unitarian clergy, however unwilling to widen the breach between themselves and the old Church, were ill at ease under the challenges of Orthodox critics, and could not escape the necessity of defining their belief.

> "According to your own concession," rejoined Dr. Samuel Worcester to Channing's letter, "the party in whose behalf you plead generally deny the essential divinity of the Saviour, and hold him to be a being entirely 'distinct from God,' entirely 'dependent,'—in other words, a mere creature.... You doubtless do not suppose that by any mere creature atonement could be made for the sins of an apostate world of sufficient merit for the pardon, sanctification, and eternal salvation of all who should trust in him; therefore if you hold to atonement in any sense, yet unquestionably not in the sense of a proper propitiatory

sacrifice. Upon this denial of atonement must follow of course the denial of pardon procured by the blood of Christ, of justification through faith in him, of redemption from eternal death unto everlasting life by him. Connected, and generally if not invariably concomitant, with the denial of these doctrines is a denial of the Holy Spirit in his personal character and offices, and of the renewal of mankind unto holiness by his sovereign agency, as held by Orthodox Christians. Now, sir, are these small and trivial points of difference between you and us?"

Channing protested against these inferences; but he did not deny—indeed, he affirmed—that Unitarians regarded dogma as unnecessary to salvation. "In our judgment of professed Christians," he replied, "we are guided more by their temper and lives than by any peculiarities of opinion. We lay it down as a great and indisputable opinion, clear as the sun at noonday, that the great end for which Christian truth is revealed is the sanctification of the soul, the formation of the Christian character; and wherever we see the marks of this character displayed in a professed disciple of Jesus, we hope, and rejoice to hope, that he has received all the truth which is necessary to his salvation." The hope might help to soothe anxiety and distress, but it defied conclusions reached by the most anxious and often renewed labors of churchmen for eighteen hundred years. Something more than a hope was necessary as the foundation of a faith.

Not until the year 1819, did Channing quit the cautious attitude he at first assumed. Then, in his "Sermon on the Ordination of Jared Sparks" at Baltimore, he accepted the obligation to define his relation to Christian doctrine, and with the support of Andrews Norton, Henry Ware, and other Unitarian clergymen gave a doctrinal character to the movement. With this phase of his influence the present story has nothing to do.

In the intellectual development of the country, the earlier stage of Unitarianism was more interesting than the later, for it marked a general tendency of national thought. At a time when Boston grew little in population and but moderately in wealth, and when it was regarded with antipathy, both political and religious, by a vast majority of the American people, its society had never been so agreeable or so fecund. No such display of fresh and winning genius had yet been seen in America as was offered by the genial outburst of intellectual activity in the early days of the Unitarian schism. No more was heard of the Westminster doctrine that man had lost all ability of will to any spiritual good accompanying salvation, but was dead in sin. So strong was the reaction against old dogmas that for thirty years society seemed less likely to resume the ancient faith in the Christian Trinity than to establish a new Trinity, in which a deified humanity should have place. Under the influence of Channing and his friends, human nature was adorned with virtues hardly suspected before, and with hopes of perfection on earth altogether strange to theology. The Church then charmed. The worth of man became under Channing's teachings a source of pride and joy, with such insistence as to cause his hearers at last to recall, almost with a sense of relief, that the Saviour himself had been content to regard them only as of more value than many sparrows.

The most remarkable quality of Unitarianism was its high social and intellectual character. The other more popular religious movements followed for the most part a less ambitious path, but were marked by the same humanitarian tendency. In contrast with old stringency of thought, the religious activity of the epoch showed warmth of emotion. The elder Buckminster, a consistent Calvinist clergyman, settled at Portsmouth in New Hampshire, while greatly distressed by his son's leanings toward loose theology, was at the same time obliged to witness the success of other opinions, which he thought monstrous, preached by Hosea Ballou, an active minister in the same town. This new doctrine, which took the name of Universalism, held as an article of faith "that there is one God, whose nature is love, revealed in one Lord Jesus Christ, by one Holy Spirit of grace, who will finally restore the whole family of mankind to holiness and happiness." In former times any one who had publicly professed belief in universal salvation would not have been regarded as a Christian. With equal propriety he might have preached the divinity of Ammon or Diana. To the old theology one god was as strange as the other; and so deeply impressed was Dr. Buckminster with this conviction, that he felt himself constrained in the year 1809 to warn Hosea Ballou of his error, in a letter pathetic for its conscientious self-restraint. Yet the Universalists steadily grew in numbers and respectability, spreading from State to State under Ballou's guidance, until they became as well-established and as respectable a church as that to which Buckminster belonged.

A phenomenon still more curious was seen in the same year, 1809, in western Pennsylvania. Near the banks of the Monongahela, in Washington County, a divergent branch of Scotch Presbyterianism established a small church, and under the guidance of Thomas Campbell, a recent emigrant from Scotland, issued, Sept. 7, 1809, a Declaration:

"Being well aware from sad experience of the heinous nature and pernicious tendency of religious controversy among Christians, tired and sick of the bitter jarrings and janglings of a party spirit, we would desire to be at rest; and were it possible, would also desire to adopt and recommend such measures as would give rest to our brethren throughout all the churches, as would restore unity, peace, and purity to the whole Church of God. This desirable rest, however, we utterly despair either to find for ourselves, or to be able to recommend to our brethren, by continuing amid the diversity and rancor of party contentions the varying uncertainty and clashings of human opinions; nor indeed can we reasonably expect to find it anywhere but in Christ and his simple word, which is the same yesterday, to-day, and forever. Our desire, therefore, for ourselves and our brethren would be that rejecting human opinions and the inventions of men as of any authority, or as having any place in the Church of God, we might forever cease from further contentions about such things, returning to and holding fast by the original standard."

Campbell's Declaration expressed so wide a popular want that his church, in a few years, became one of the largest branches of the great Baptist persuasion. Perhaps in these instances of rapid popular grouping, love of peace was to some extent supplemented by jealousy of learning, and showed as much spirit of social independence as of religious instinct. The growth of vast popular sects in a democratic community might testify to intellectual stagnation as well as to religious or social earnestness; but whatever was the amount of thought involved in such movements, one character was common to them all, as well as to the Unitarians,—they agreed in relaxing the strictness of theological reasoning. Channing united with Campbell in suggesting that the Church should ignore what it could not comprehend. In a popular and voluntary form they proposed self-restraints which should have the same effect as the formal restraints of the hierarchies. "Rejecting," like Campbell, "human opinions and the inventions of men,"—preaching, like Channing and Ballou, "that there is one God, whose nature is love," and that doctrine was useless except to promote a spirit of love,—they founded new churches on what seemed to resemble an argument that the intellectual difficulties in their path must be unessential because they were insuperable.

Wide as the impulse was to escape the rigor of bonds and re-lax the severity of thought, organizations so deeply founded as the old churches were not capable of destruction. They had seen many similar human efforts, and felt certain that sooner or later such experiments must end in a return to the old stan-dards. Even the Congregational Church of New England, though reduced in Boston to a shadow of its old authority, maintained itself at large against its swarm of enemies,—Uni-tarian, Universalist, Baptist, Methodist,—resisting, with force of character and reasoning, the looseness of doctrine and vagueness of thought which marked the time. Yale College re-mained true to it. Most of the parishes maintained their old re-lations. If the congregations in some instances crumbled away or failed to increase, the Church could still stand erect, and might reflect with astonishment on its own strength, which survived so long a series of shocks apparently fatal. For half a century the Congregational clergy had struggled to prevent in-novation, while the people emigrated by hundreds of thou-sands in order to innovate. Obliged to insist on the infinite justice rather than on the infinite mercy of God, they shocked the instincts of the new generation, which wanted to enjoy worldly blessings without fear of future reckoning. Driven to bay by the deistic and utilitarian principles of Jefferson's demo-cracy, they fell into the worldly error of defying the national in-stinct, pressing their resistance to the war until it amounted to treasonable conspiracy. The sudden peace swept away much that was respectable in the old society of America, but perhaps its noblest victim was the unity of the New England Church.

The Church, whether Catholic or Protestant, Lutheran or Calvinistic, always rested in the conviction that every diver-gence from the great highways of religious thought must be temporary, and that no permanent church was possible except on foundations already established; but the State stood in a po-sition less self-confident. The old principles of government were less carefully developed, and Democrats in politics were more certain than Unitarians or Universalists in theology that their intellectual conclusions made a stride in the progress of thought. Yet the sixteen years with which the century opened were singularly barren of new political ideas. Apparently the extreme activity which marked the political speculations of the period between 1775 and 1800, both in America and in Europe, had exhausted the energy of society, for Americans showed interest only in the practical working of their experiments, and added nothing to the ideas that underlay them. With such political thought as society produced, these pages have been chiefly filled; the result has been told. The same tendency which in religion led to reaction against dogma, was shown in politics by general acquiescence in practices which left unsettled the disputed principles of government. No one could say with confidence what theory of the Constitution had prevailed. Neither party was satisfied, although both acquiesced. While the Legislative and Executive branches of the government acted on no fixed principle, but established precedents at variance with any consistent theory, the Judiciary rendered so few decisions that Constitutional law stood nearly still. Only at a later time did Chief-Justice Marshall begin his great series of judicial opinions,—McCulloch against the State of Maryland in 1819; Dartmouth College in the same year; Cohens against the State of Virginia in 1821. No sooner were these decisive rulings announced, than they roused the last combative energies of Jefferson against his old enemy the Judiciary: "That body, like gravity, ever acting, with noiseless foot and unalarming advance, gaining ground step by step, and holding what it gains, is engulfing insidiously the special governments."

Marshall had few occasions to decide Constitutional points during the Administrations of Jefferson and Madison, but the opinions he gave were emphatic. When Pennsylvania in 1809 resisted, in the case of Gideon Olmstead, a process of the

Supreme Court, the chief-justice, without unnecessary words, declared that "if the legislatures of the several States may at will annul the judgments of the courts of the United States, and destroy the rights acquired under those judgments, the Constitution itself becomes a solemn mockery, and the nation is deprived of the means of enforcing its laws by the instrumentality of its own tribunals." Pennsylvania yielded; and Marshall, in the following year, carried a step further the authority of his court. He overthrew the favorite dogma of John Randolph and the party of States rights, so long and vehemently maintained in the Yazoo dispute.

The Yazoo claims came before the court in the case of Fletcher against Peck, argued first in 1809 by Luther Martin, J. Q. Adams, and Robert G. Harper; and again in 1810 by Martin, Harper, and Joseph Story. March 16, 1810, the chief-justice delivered the opinion. Declining, as "indecent in the extreme," to enter into an inquiry as to the corruption of "the sovereign power of a State," he dealt with the issue whether a legislature could annul rights vested in an individual by a law in its nature a contract.

> "It may well be doubted," he argued, "whether the nature of society and government does not prescribe some limits to the legislative power; and if any are to be prescribed, where are they to be found if the property of an individual, fairly and honestly acquired, may be seized without compensation? To the legislature all legislative power is granted; but the question whether the act of transferring the property of an individual to the public be in the nature of the legislative power, is well worthy of serious reflection. It is the peculiar province of the legislature to prescribe general rules for the government of society: the application of those rules to individuals in society would seem to be the duty of other departments. How far the

power of giving the law may involve every other power, in cases where the Constitution is silent, never has been and perhaps never can be definitely stated."

In the case under consideration, Marshall held that the Constitution was not silent. The provision that no State could pass any law impairing the obligation of contracts, as well as "the general principles which are common to our free institutions," restrained the State of Georgia from passing a law whereby the previous contract could be rendered void. His decision settled, as far as concerned the Judiciary, a point regarded as vital by the States-rights school. Four years afterward Congress gave the required compensation for the contract broken by Georgia.

The chief-justice rendered no more leading Constitutional decisions during Madison's term of office; but his influence was seen in a celebrated opinion delivered by Justice Story in 1816, in the case of Martin against Hunter's Lessee. There the court came in conflict with the State of Virginia. The Court of Appeals of that State refused to obey a mandate of the Supreme Court, alleging that the proceedings of the Supreme Court were *coram non judice*, or beyond its jurisdiction, being founded on section 25 of the Judiciary Act of 1789, which was unconstitutional in extending the appellate jurisdiction of the Supreme Court over the State courts.

The Court of Appeals was unfortunate in the moment of its resistance to the authority of the national courts. While the case was passing through its last stage peace was declared, and the national authority sprang into vigor unknown before. The chief-justice would not with his own hand humiliate the pride of the Court of Appeals, for which as a Virginian and a lawyer he could feel only deep respect. He devolved the unpleasant duty on young Justice Story, whose own State of Massachusetts was then far from being an object of jealousy to Virginia, and who, a Republican in politics, could not be prejudiced by party feeling against the Virginia doctrine. Much of the opinion bore the stamp of Marshall's mind; much showed the turn of Story's intelligence; yet the same principle lay beneath the whole, and no one could detect a divergence between the Federalism of the Virginia chief-justice and the Democracy of the Massachusetts lawyer.

> "It has been argued," said the court, "that such an appellate jurisdiction over State courts is inconsistent with the genius of our governments and the spirit of the Constitution; that the latter was never designed to act upon State sovereignties, but only upon the people; and that if the power exists, it will materially impair the sovereignty of the States and the independence of their courts. We cannot yield to the force of this reasoning; it assumes principles which we cannot admit, and draws conclusions to which we do not yield our assent. It is a mistake that the Constitution was not designed to operate upon States in their corporate capacity. It is crowded with provisions which restrain or annul the sovereignty of the States in some of the highest branches of their prerogatives. . . . When, therefore, the States are stripped of some of the highest attributes of sovereignty, and the same are given to the United States; when the legislatures of the States are in some respects under the control of Congress, and in every case are, under the Constitution, bound by the paramount authority of the United States,—it is certainly difficult to support the argument that the appellate power over the decisions of State courts is contrary to the genius of our institutions."

So far were the political principles of the people from having united in a common understanding, that while the Supreme

Court of the United States thus differed from the Virginia Court of Appeals in regard to the genius of the government and the spirit of the Constitution, Jefferson still publicly maintained that the national and state governments were "as independent, in fact, as different nations," and that the function of one was foreign, while that of the other was domestic. Madison still declared that Congress could not build a road or clear a watercourse; while Congress believed itself authorized to do both, and in that belief passed a law which Madison vetoed. In politics as in theology, the practical system which resulted from sixteen years of experience seemed to rest on the agreement not to press principles to a conclusion.

No new idea was brought forward, and the old ideas, though apparently incapable of existing together, continued to exist in rivalry like that of the dogmas which perplexed the theological world; but between the political and religious movement a distinct difference could be seen. The Church showed no tendency to unite in any creed or dogma,—indeed, religious society rather tended to more divisions; but in politics public opinion slowly moved in a fixed direction. The movement could not easily be measured, and was subject to reaction; but its reality was shown by the protests of Jefferson, the veto of Madison, and the decisions of the Supreme Court. No one doubted that a change had occurred since 1798. The favorite States-rights dogma of that time had suffered irreparable injury. For sixteen years the national government in all its branches had acted, without listening to remonstrance, on the rule that it was the rightful interpreter of its own powers. In this assumption the Executive, the Legislature, and the Judiciary had agreed. Massachusetts and Pennsylvania, as well as Virginia and Georgia, yielded. Louisiana had been bought and admitted into the Union; the Embargo had been enforced; one National Bank had been destroyed and another established; every essential function of a sovereignty had been performed, without an

instance of failure, though not without question. However unwilling the minority might be to admit in theory the overthrow
of their principles, every citizen assented in daily practice to the
rule that the national government alone interpreted its own
powers in the last resort. From the moment the whole people
learned to accept the practice, the dispute over theory lost importance, and the Virginia Resolutions of 1798 marked only a
stage in the development of a sovereignty.

The nature of the sovereignty that was to be the result of
American political experiment, the amount of originality
which could be infused into an idea so old, was a matter for future history to settle. Many years were likely to elapse before
the admitted practice of the government and people could be
fully adopted into the substance of their law, but the process
thus far had been rapid. In the brief space of thirty years, between 1787 and 1817,—a short generation,—the Union had
passed through astonishing stages. Probably no great people
ever grew more rapidly and became more mature in so short a
time. The ideas of 1787 were antiquated in 1815, and lingered
only in districts remote from active movement. The subsidence
of interest in political theories was a measure of the change,
marking the general drift of society toward practical devices for
popular use, within popular intelligence. The only work that
could be said to represent a school of thought in politics was
written by John Taylor of Caroline, and was probably never
read,—or if read, certainly never understood,—north of
Baltimore by any but curious and somewhat deep students, although to them it had value.

John Taylor of Caroline might without irreverence be described as a *vox clamantis*,—the voice of one crying in the
wilderness. Regarded as a political thinker of the first rank by
Jefferson, Monroe, John Randolph, and the Virginia school, he
admitted, with the geniality of the class to which he belonged,
that his disciples invariably deserted in practice the rules they

praised in his teaching; but he continued to teach, and the further his scholars drifted from him the more publicly and profusely he wrote. His first large volume, "An Inquiry into the Principles and Policy of the Government of the United States," published in 1814, during the war, was in form an answer to John Adams's "Defence of the Constitutions" published in London twenty-five years before. In 1787 John Adams, like Jefferson, Hamilton, Madison, Jay, and other constitution-makers, might, without losing the interest of readers, indulge in speculations more or less visionary in regard to the future character of a nation yet in its cradle; but in 1814 the character of people and government was formed; the lines of their activity were fixed. A people which had in 1787 been indifferent or hostile to roads, banks, funded debt, and nationality, had become in 1815 habituated to ideas and machinery of the sort on a great scale. Monarchy or aristocracy no longer entered into the public mind as factors in future development. Yet Taylor resumed the discussions of 1787 as though the interval were a blank; and his only conclusion from the experience of thirty years was that both political parties were equally moving in a wrong direction.

> "The two parties, called Republican and Federal," he concluded, "have hitherto undergone but one revolution. Yet each when in power preached Filmer's old doctrine of passive obedience in a new form, with considerable success; and each, out of power, strenuously controverted it. The party in power asserted that however absurd or slavish this doctrine was under other forms of the numerical analysis, the people under ours were *identified* (the new term to cog this old doctrine upon the United States) with the government; and that therefore an opposition to the government was an opposition to the nation itself. . . . This identifying doctrine . . . puts an end to the idea of

a responsibility of the government to the nation; . . . it renders useless the freedom of speech and of the press; it converts the representative into the principal; it destroys the division of power between the people and the government, as being themselves indivisible; and in short it is inconsistent with every principle by which politicians and philosophers have hitherto defined a free government."

The principle to which Taylor so strenuously objected was nevertheless the chief political result of national experience. Somewhere or another a point was always reached where opposition became treasonable,—as Virginia, like Massachusetts, had learned both when in power and when out. Taylor's speculations ended only in an admission of their own practical sterility, and his suggestions for restraining the growth of authority assumed the possibility of returning to the conditions of 1787. Banks were his horror. Stocks and bonds, or paper evidences of indebtedness in any form, he thought destructive to sound principles of government. The Virginia and Kentucky Resolutions of 1798 were his best resource for the preservation of civil liberty. However well-founded his fears might be, his correctives could no longer be applied. Political philosophers of all ages were fond of devising systems for imaginary Republics, Utopias, and Oceanas, where practical difficulties could not stand in their way. Taylor was a political philosopher of the same school, and his Oceana on the banks of the Rappahannock was a reflection of his own virtues.

Literature and Art

SOCIETY showed great interest in the statesmen or preachers who won its favor, and earnestly discussed the value of political or religious dogmas, without betraying a wish to subject itself ever again to the rigor of a strict creed in politics or religion. In a similar spirit it touched here and there, with a light hand, the wide circuit of what was called *belles lettres*, without showing severity either in taste or temper.

For the first four or five years of the century, Dennie's "Portfolio" contained almost everything that was produced in the United States under the form of light literature. The volumes of the "Portfolio" for that period had the merit of representing the literary efforts of the time, for Philadelphia insisted on no standard of taste so exacting as to exclude merit, or even dulness, in any literary form. Jacobins, as Dennie called Democrats, were not admitted into the circle of the "Portfolio;" but Jacobins rarely troubled themselves with *belles lettres*.

The "Portfolio" reflected a small literary class scattered throughout the country, remarkable chiefly for close adhesion to established English ideas. The English standard was then extravagantly Tory, and the American standard was the same. At first sight the impression was strange. A few years later, no ordinary reader could remember that ideas so illiberal had seriously prevailed among educated Americans. By an effort, elderly men could, in the next generation, recall a time when they had been taught that Oliver Cromwell was a monster of wickedness and hypocrisy; but they could hardly believe that at any period an American critic coldly qualified "Paradise Lost," and "Avenge, O Lord, thy slaughtered saints," as good poetry, though written by a Republican and an enemy of established order. This was the tone of Dennie's criticism, and so little was it confined to him that even young Buckminster, in his Phi Beta Kappa Oration of 1809, which was regarded as making almost an epoch in American literature, spoke of Milton's eyes as "quenched in the service of a vulgar and usurping faction," and of Milton's life as "a memorable instance of the temporary degradation of learning." Buckminster was then remonstrating against the influence of politics upon letters rather than expressing a political sentiment, but his illustration was colored by the general prejudices of British Toryism. Half a century before, Dr. Johnson had taken the tone of Tory patronage toward Milton's genius, and Johnson and Burke were still received in America as final authorities for correct opinion in morals, literature, and politics. The "Portfolio" regarded Johnson not only as a "superlative" moralist and politician, but also as a "sublime" critic and a "transcendent" poet. Burke and Cicero stood on the same level, as masters before whose authority criticism must silently bow.

Yet side by side with these conventional standards, the "Portfolio" showed tendencies which seemed inconsistent with conservatism,—a readiness to welcome literary innovations contradicting every established canon. No one would have supposed that the critic who accepted Johnson and Pope as transcendent poets, should also delight in Burns and Wordsworth; yet Dennie was unstinted in praise of poetry which, as literature, was hardly less revolutionary than the writings of Godwin in politics. Dennie lost no opportunity of praising Coleridge, and reprinted with enthusiasm the simplest ballads of Wordsworth. Moore was his personal friend, and Moore's verses his models. Wherever his political prejudices were untouched, he

loved novelty. He seemed to respect classical authority only because it was established, but his literary instincts were broader
than those of Jefferson.

The original matter of the "Portfolio" was naturally un-
equal, and for the most part hardly better than that of a college
magazine. Dennie was apt to be commonplace, trivial, and
dull. His humor was heavy and commonly coarse; he allowed
himself entire freedom, and no little grossness of taste. Of
scholarship, or scholarly criticism, his paper showed great want.
He tried to instruct as well as to amuse, but society soon passed
the stage to which his writing belonged. The circulation of the
"Portfolio" probably never exceeded fifteen hundred copies,
and Dennie constantly complained that the paper barely supported itself. When the Bostonians, in the year 1805, began to
feel the spirit of literary ambition, they took at once a stride beyond Dennie's power, and established a monthly magazine
called the "Anthology and Boston Review," which in 1806
numbered four hundred and forty subscribers. The undertaking was doubly remarkable; for the Anthology Society which
supported the Review combined with it the collection of a library, limited at first to periodical publications, which ex-
panded slowly into the large and useful library known as the
Boston Athenæum. The Review and Library quickly became
the centre of literary taste in Boston, and, in the words of
Josiah Quincy many years afterward, might be considered as a
revival of polite learning in America. The claim was not unrea-
sonable, for the Review far surpassed any literary standards
then existing in the United States, and was not much inferior
to any in England; for the Edinburgh was established only in
1802, and the Quarterly not till 1809.

The Anthology Society, which accomplished the feat of giving to Boston for the first time the lead of American literary effort, consisted largely of clergymen, and represented, perhaps
unintentionally, the coming Unitarian movement. Its president

and controlling spirit had no sympathy with either division of the Congregational Church, but was a clergyman of the Church of England. John Sylvester John Gardiner, the rector of Trinity, occupied a peculiar position in Boston. Of American descent, but English birth and education, he was not prevented by the isolation of his clerical character from taking an active part in affairs, and his activity was sometimes greater than his discretion. His political sermons rivalled those of the Congregational ministers Osgood and Parish, in their violence against Jefferson and the national government; his Federalism was that of the Essex Junto, with a more decided leaning to disunion; but he was also an active and useful citizen, ready to take his share in every good work. When he became president of the Anthology Society, he was associated with a clergyman of Unitarian opinions as vice-president,—the Rev. William Emerson, a man of high reputation in his day, but better known in after years as the father of Ralph Waldo Emerson. The first editor was Samuel Cooper Thacher, to whom, ten years afterward, Channing addressed his earliest controversial letter. Young Buckminster and William Tudor, a Boston man, who for the next twenty years was active in the literary life of Massachusetts, were also original members. The staff of the "Anthology" was greatly superior to ordinary editorial resources; and in a short time the Review acquired a reputation for ability and sharpness of temper never wholly forgiven. Its unpopularity was the greater because its aggressiveness took the form of assaults on Calvinism, which earned the ill-will of the Congregational clergy.

Buckminster and Channing were the editor's closest friends, and their liberality of thought was remarkable for the time and place; yet the point from which the liberality of Boston started would have been regarded in most parts of the Union as conservative. Channing's fear of France and attachment to England were superstitious.

"I will not say," began his Fast Day Sermon in 1810, "that the present age is as strongly marked or distinguished from all other ages as that in which Jesus Christ appeared; but with that single exception, perhaps the present age is the most eventful the world has ever known. We live in times which have no parallel in past ages; in times when the human character has almost assumed a new form; in times of peculiar calamity, of thick darkness, and almost of despair. . . . The danger is so vast, so awful, and so obvious, that the blindness, the indifference, which prevail argue infatuation, and give room for apprehension that nothing can rouse us to those efforts by which alone the danger can be averted. Am I asked what there is so peculiar and so tremendous in the times in which we live? . . . I answer: In the very heart of Europe, in the centre of the civilized world, a new power has suddenly arisen on the ruins of old institutions, peculiar in its character, and most ruinous in its influence."

While Channing felt for France the full horror of his Federalist principles, he regarded England with equivalent affection.

"I feel a peculiar interest in England," he explained in a note appended to the Fast Day Sermon; "for I believe that there Christianity is exerting its best influences on the human character; that there the perfections of human nature, wisdom, virtue, and piety are fostered by excellent institutions, and are producing the delightful fruits of domestic happiness, social order, and general prosperity."

The majority of Americans took a different view of the subject; but even those who most strongly agreed with Channing would have been first to avow that their prejudice was inveterate, and its consequences sweeping. Such a conviction admitted

little room for liberalism where politics were, directly or re-
motely, involved. Literature bordered closely on politics, and
the liberalism of Unitarian Boston was bounded even in literature by the limits of British sympathies. Buckminster's Phi Beta
Kappa Oration of 1809 was as emphatic on this point as Channing's Fast Day Sermon of 1810 was outspoken in its political
antipathies.

> "It is our lot," said Buckminster, "to have been born in an
> age of tremendous revolution, and the world is yet cov-
> ered with the wrecks of its ancient glory, especially of its
> literary renown. The fury of that storm which rose in
> France is passed and spent, but its effects have been felt
> through the whole system of liberal education. The foul
> spirit of innovation and sophistry has been seen wander-
> ing in the very groves of the Lyceum, and is not yet com-
> pletely exorcised, though the spell is broken."

The liberalism of Boston began in a protest against "the foul
spirit of innovation," and could hardly begin at any point more
advanced. "Infidelity has had one triumph in our days, and we
have seen learning as well as virtue trampled under the hoofs of
its infuriated steeds, let loose by the hand of impiety." From
this attitude of antipathy to innovation, the Unitarian movement began its attempts to innovate, and with astonishing rapidity passed through phases which might well have required
ages of growth. In five years Channing began open attack upon
the foundation, or what had hitherto been believed the foundation, of the Church; and from that moment innovation could
no longer be regarded as foul.

Of the intellectual movement in all its new directions,
Harvard College was the centre. Between 1805 and 1817 the college inspired the worn-out Federalism of Boston with life till
then unimagined. Not only did it fill the pulpits with Buck-

minsters, Channings, and Thachers, whose sermons were an unfailing interest, and whose society was a constant stimulus, but it also maintained a rivalry between the pulpit and the lecture-room. The choice of a new professor was as important and as much discussed as the choice of a new minister. No ordinary political event caused more social interest than the appointment of Henry Ware as Professor of Theology in 1805. In the following year J. Q. Adams was made Professor of Rhetoric, and delivered a course of lectures, which created the school of oratory to which Edward Everett's generation adhered. Four younger men, whose influence was greatly felt in their branches of instruction, received professorships in the next few years,— Jacob Bigelow, who was appointed Professor of Medicine in 1813; Edward Everett, Greek Professor in 1815; John Collins Warren, Professor of Anatomy in the same year; and George Ticknor, Professor of *Belles Lettres* in 1816. In the small society of Boston, a city numbering hardly forty thousand persons, this activity of college and church produced a new era. Where thirty-nine students a year had entered the college before 1800, an average number of sixty-six entered it during the war, and took degrees during the four or five subsequent years. Among them were names familiar to the literature and politics of the next half century. Besides Ticknor and Everett, in 1807 and 1811, Henry Ware graduated in 1812, and his brother William, the author of "Zenobia," in 1816; William Hickling Prescott, in 1814; J. G. Palfrey, in 1815; in 1817, George Bancroft and Caleb Cushing graduated, and Ralph Waldo Emerson entered the college. Boston also drew resources from other quarters, and perhaps showed no stronger proof of its vigor than when, in 1816, it attracted Daniel Webster from New Hampshire to identify himself with the intellect and interests of Massachusetts. Even by reaction the Unitarians stimulated Boston,—as when, a few years afterward, Lyman Beecher accepted the charge of a Boston church in order to resist their encroachments.

The "Anthology," which marked the birth of the new literary school, came in a few years to a natural end, but was revived in 1815 under the name of the "North American Review," by the exertions of William Tudor. The life of the new Review belonged to a later period, and was shaped by other influences than those that surrounded the "Anthology." With the beginning of the next epoch, the provincial stage of the Boston school was closed. More and more its influence tended to become national, and even to affect other countries. Perhaps by a natural consequence rather than by coincidence, the close of the old period was marked by the appearance of a short original poem in the "North American Review" for September, 1817:—

> "... The hills,
> Rock-ribbed and ancient as the sun; the vales
> Stretching in pensive quietness between;
> The venerable woods; the floods that move
> In majesty, and the complaining brooks
> That wind among the meads and make them green,—
> Are but the solemn declarations all,
> Of the great tomb of man. The golden sun,
> The planets, all the infinite host of heaven
> Are glowing on the sad abodes of death
> Through the still lapse of ages. All that tread
> The globe are but a handful to the tribes
> That slumber in its bosom. Take the wings
> Of morning, and the Borean desert pierce;
> Or lose thyself in the continuous woods
> That veil Oregan, where he hears no sound
> Save his own dashings,—yet the dead are there;
> And millions in these solitudes, since first
> The flight of years began, have laid them down
> In their last sleep: the dead reign there alone.
> So shalt thou rest: and what if thou shalt fall

Unnoticed by the living, and no friend
Take note of thy departure? Thousands more
Will share thy destiny. The tittering world
Dance to the grave. The busy brood of care
Plod on, and each one chases as before
His favorite phantom. Yet all these shall leave
Their mirth and their employments, and shall come
And make their bed with thee."

The appearance of "Thanatopsis" and "Lines to a Waterfowl" in the early numbers of the "North American Review," while leaving no doubt that a new national literature was close at hand, proved also that it was not to be the product of a single source; for Bryant, though greatly tempted to join the Emersons, Channing, Dana, Allston, and Tudor in Boston, turned finally to New York, where influences of a different kind surrounded him. The Unitarian school could not but take a sober cast, and even its humor was sure to be tinged with sadness, sarcasm, or irony, or some serious purpose or passion; but New York contained no atmosphere in which such a society could thrive. Busy with the charge of practical work,—the development of industries continually exceeding their power of control,—the people of New York wanted amusement, and shunned what in Boston was considered as intellectual. Their tastes were gratified by the appearance of a writer whose first book created a school of literature as distinctly marked as the Unitarian school of Boston, and more decidedly original. "The History of New York, by Diedrich Knickerbocker," appeared in 1809, and stood alone. Other books of the time seemed to recognize some literary parentage. Channing and Buckminster were links in a chain of theologians and preachers. "Thanatopsis" evidently drew inspiration from Wordsworth. Diedrich Knickerbocker owed nothing to any living original.

The "History of New York" was worth more than passing

notice. In the development of a national character, as well as of the literature that reflected it, humor was a trait of the utmost interest; and Washington Irving was immediately recognized as a humorist whose name, if he fulfilled the promise of his first attempt, would have a chance of passing into the society of Rabelais, Cervantes, Butler, and Sterne. Few literary tasks were more difficult than to burlesque without vulgarizing, and to satirize without malignity; yet Irving in his first effort succeeded in doing both. The old families, and serious students of colonial history, never quite forgave Irving for throwing an atmosphere of ridicule over the subject of their interest; but Diedrich Knickerbocker's History was so much more entertaining than ordinary histories, that even historians could be excused for regretting that it should not be true.

Yet the book reflected the political passions which marked the period of the Embargo. Besides the burlesque, the "History" contained satire; and perhaps its most marked trait was the good-nature which, at a time when bitterness was universal in politics, saved Irving's political satire from malignity. Irving meant that no one should mistake the character of the universal genius, Governor Wilhelmus Kieft, surnamed the Testy, who as a youth had made many curious investigations into the nature and operations of windmills, and who came well-nigh being smothered in a slough of unintelligible learning,—"a fearful peril, from the effects of which he never perfectly recovered."

"No sooner had this bustling little man been blown by a whiff of fortune into the seat of government, than he called together his council and delivered a very animated speech on the affairs of the government; . . . and here he soon worked himself into a fearful rage against the Yankees, whom he compared to the Gauls who desolated Rome, and to the Goths and Vandals who overran the fairest plains of Europe. . . . Having thus artfully wrought

up his tale of terror to a climax, he assumed a self-satis-
fied look, and declared with a nod of knowing import
that he had taken measures to put a final stop to these encroachments,—that he had been obliged to have recourse
to a dreadful engine of warfare, lately invented, awful in
its effects but authorized by direful necessity; in a word,
he was resolved to conquer the Yankees—by Proclamation."

Washington Irving's political relations were those commonly
known as Burrite, through his brother Peter, who edited in
Burr's interest the "Morning Chronicle." Antipathy to Jefferson
was a natural result, and Irving's satire on the President was the
more interesting because the subject offered temptations for ill-
tempered sarcasm such as spoiled Federalist humor. The
Knickerbocker sketch of Jefferson was worth comparing with
Federalist modes of expressing the same ideas:—

"The great defect of Wilhelmus Kieft's policy was that
though no man could be more ready to stand forth in an
hour of emergency, yet he was so intent upon guarding
the national pocket that he suffered the enemy to break
its head. . . . All this was a remote consequence of his education at the Hague; where, having acquired a smattering
of knowledge, he was ever a great conner of indexes, continually dipping into books without ever studying to the
bottom of any subject, so that he had the scum of all
kinds of authors fermenting in his pericranium. In some
of these titlepage researches he unluckily stumbled over a
grand political *cabalistic word,* which with his customary
facility he immediately incorporated into his great
scheme of government, to the irretrievable injury and
delusion of the honest province of Nieuw Nederlands,
and the eternal misleading of all experimental rulers."

Little was wanting to make such a sketch bitter; but Irving seemed to have the power of deadening venom by a mere trick of hand. Readers of the "History," after a few years had passed, rarely remembered the satire, or supposed that the story contained it. The humor and the style remained to characterize a school.

The originality of the Knickerbocker humor was the more remarkable because it was allowed to stand alone. Irving published nothing else of consequence until 1819, and then, abandoning his early style, inclined to imitate Addison and Steele, although his work was hardly the less original. Irving preceded Walter Scott, whose "Waverley" appeared in 1814, and "Guy Mannering" in 1815; and if either author could be said to influence the other, the influence of Diedrich Knickerbocker on Scott was more evident than that of "Waverley" on Irving.

In the face of the spontaneous burst of genius which at that moment gave to English literature and art a character distinct even in its own experience, Americans might have been excused for making no figure at all. Other periods produced one poet at a time, and measured originality by single poems; or satisfied their ambition by prose or painting of occasional merit. The nineteenth century began in England with genius as plenty as it was usually rare. To Beattie, Cowper, and Burns, succeeded Wordsworth, Coleridge, Scott, Byron, Crabbe, Campbell, Charles Lamb, Moore, Shelley, and Keats. The splendor of this combination threw American and even French talent into the shade, and defied hope of rivalry; but the American mind, as far as it went, showed both freshness and originality. The divergence of American from English standards seemed insignificant to critics who required, as they commonly did, a national literature founded on some new conception,—such as the Shawanee or Aztecs could be supposed to suggest; but to those who expected only a slow variation from European types, the difference was well marked. Channing and Irving were American in literature, as Calhoun and Webster were American in politics. They were the product of influences as peculiar to the country as those which produced Fulton and his steamboat.

While Bryant published "Thanatopsis" and Irving made his studies for the "Sketch-Book," another American of genius perhaps superior to theirs—Washington Allston—was painting in London, before returning to pass the remainder of his life in the neighborhood of Boston and Harvard College. Between thirty and forty years of age, Allston was then in the prime of his powers; and even in a circle of artists which included Turner, Wilkie, Mulready, Constable, Callcott, Crome, Cotman, and a swarm of others equally famous, Allston was distinguished. Other Americans took rank in the same society. Leslie and Stuart Newton were adopted into it, and Copley died only in 1815, while Trumbull painted in London till 1816; but remarkable though they were for the quality of their art, they belonged to a British school, and could be claimed as American only by blood. Allston stood in a relation somewhat different. In part, his apparent Americanism was due to his later return, and to his identification with American society; but the return itself was probably caused by a peculiar bent of character. His mind was not wholly English.

Allston's art and his originality were not such as might have been expected from an American, or such as Americans were likely to admire; and the same might be said of Leslie and Stuart Newton. Perhaps the strongest instance of all was Edward Malbone, whose grace of execution was not more remarkable than his talent for elevating the subject of his exquisite work. So far from sharing the imagination of Shawanee Indians or even of Democrats, these men instinctively reverted to the most refined and elevated schools of art. Not only did Allston show from the beginning of his career a passion for the nobler

standards of his profession, but also for technical quality,—a
taste less usual. Washington Irving met him in Rome in 1805,
when both were unknown; and they became warm friends.

> "I do not think I have ever been more captivated on a
> first acquaintance," wrote Irving long afterward. "He was
> of a light and graceful form, with large blue eyes and
> black silken hair. Everything about him bespoke the man
> of intellect and refinement.... He was exquisitely sensi-
> tive to the graceful and the beautiful, and took great de-
> light in paintings which excelled in color; yet he was
> strongly moved and aroused by objects of grandeur. I
> well recollect the admiration with which he contem-
> plated the sublime statue of Moses, by Michael Angelo."

The same tastes characterized his life, and gave to his work a
distinction that might be Italian, but was certainly not English
or usual.

"It was Allston," said Leslie, "who first awakened what little
sensibility I may possess to the beauties of color. For a long
time I took the merit of the Venetians on trust, and if left to
myself should have preferred works which I now feel to be
comparatively worthless. I remember when the picture of 'The
Ages' by Titian was first pointed out to me by Allston as an exquisite work, I thought he was laughing at me." Leslie, if not a
great colorist, was seldom incorrect; Stuart Newton had a fine
eye for color, and Malbone was emphatically a colorist; but
Allston's sensibility to color was rare among artists, and the refinement of his mind was as unusual as the delicacy of his eye.

Allston was also singular in the liberality of his sympathies.
"I am by nature, as it respects the arts, a wide liker," he said. In
Rome he became acquainted with Coleridge; and the remark of
Coleridge which seemed to make most impression on him in
their walks "under the pines of the Villa Borghese" was evi-

dently agreeable because it expressed his own feelings. "It was there he taught me this golden rule: never to judge of any work of art by its defects." His admiration for the classics did not prevent him from admiring his contemporaries; his journey through Switzerland not only showed him a new world of Nature, but also "the truth of Turner's Swiss scenes,—the poetic truth,—which none before or since have given." For a young American art-student in 1804, such sympathies were remarkable; not so much because they were correct, as because they were neither American nor English. Neither in America nor in Europe at that day could art-schools give to every young man, at the age of twenty-five, eyes to see the color of Titian, or imagination to feel the "poetic truth" of Turner.

Other painters, besides those whose names have been mentioned, were American or worked in America, as other writers besides Bryant and Irving, and other preachers besides Buckminster and Channing, were active in their professions; but for national comparisons, types alone serve. In the course of sixteen years certain Americans became distinguished. Among these, suitable for types, were Calhoun and Clay in Congress, Pinkney and Webster at the bar, Buckminster and Channing in the pulpit, Bryant and Irving in literature, Allston and Malbone in painting. These men varied greatly in character and qualities. Some possessed strength, and some showed more delicacy than vigor; some were humorists, and some were incapable of a thought that was not serious; but all were marked by a keen sense of form and style. So little was this quality expected, that the world inclined to regard them as un-American because of their refinement. Frenchmen and Italians, and even Englishmen who knew nothing of America but its wildness, were disappointed that American oratory should be only a variation from Fox and Burke; that American literature should reproduce Steele and Wordsworth; and that American art should, at its first bound, go back to the ideals of Raphael and Titian.

The incongruity was evident. The Americans themselves called persistently for a statesmanship, religion, literature, and art which should be American; and they made a number of experiments to produce what they thought their ideals. In substance they continued to approve nothing which was not marked by style as its chief merit. The oratory of Webster and Calhoun, and even of John Randolph bore the same general and common character of style. The poetry of Bryant, the humor of Irving, the sermons of Channing, and the painting of Allston were the objects of permanent approval to the national mind. Style remained its admiration, even when every newspaper protested against the imitation of outworn forms. Dennie and Jefferson, agreeing in nothing else, agreed in this; the South Carolinian Allston saw color as naturally as the New Englander Bryant heard rhythm; and a people which seemed devoid of sense or standards of beauty, showed more ambition than older societies to acquire both.

Nothing seemed more certain than that the Americans were not artistic, that they had as a people little instinct of beauty; but their intelligence in its higher as in its lower forms was both quick and refined. Such literature and art as they produced, showed qualities akin to those which produced the swift-sailing schooner, the triumph of naval architecture. If the artistic instinct weakened, the quickness of intelligence increased.

American Character

UNTIL 1815 nothing in the future of the American Union was regarded as settled. As late as January, 1815, division into several nationalities was still thought to be possible. Such a destiny, repeating the usual experience of history, was not necessarily more unfortunate than the career of a single nationality wholly American; for if the effects of divided nationality were certain to be unhappy, those of a single society with equal certainty defied experience or sound speculation. One uniform and harmonious system appealed to the imagination as a triumph of human progress, offering prospects of peace and ease, contentment and philanthropy, such as the world had not seen; but it invited dangers, formidable because unusual or altogether unknown. The corruption of such a system might prove to be proportionate with its dimensions, and uniformity might lead to evils as serious as were commonly ascribed to diversity.

The laws of human progress were matter not for dogmatic faith, but for study; and although society instinctively regarded small States, with their clashing interests and incessant wars, as the chief obstacle to improvement, such progress as the world knew had been coupled with those drawbacks. The few examples offered by history of great political societies, relieved from external competition or rivalry, were not commonly thought encouraging. War had been the severest test of political and social character, laying bare whatever was feeble, and calling out whatever was strong; and the effect of removing such a test was an untried problem.

In 1815 for the first time Americans ceased to doubt the path they were to follow. Not only was the unity of their nation established, but its probable divergence from older societies was also well defined. Already in 1817 the difference between Europe and America was decided. In politics the distinction was more evident than in social, religious, literary, or scientific directions; and the result was singular. For a time the aggressions of England and France forced the United States into a path that seemed to lead toward European methods of government; but the popular resistance, or inertia, was so great that the most popular party leaders failed to overcome it, and no sooner did foreign dangers disappear than the system began to revert to American practices; the national government tried to lay aside its assumed powers. When Madison vetoed the bill for internal improvements he could have had no other motive than that of restoring to the government, as far as possible, its original American character.

The result was not easy to understand in theory or to make efficient in practice; but while the drift of public opinion, and still more of practical necessity, drew the government slowly toward the European standard of true political sovereignty, nothing showed that the compromise, which must probably serve the public purpose, was to be European in form or feeling. As far as politics supplied a test, the national character had already diverged from any foreign type. Opinions might differ whether the political movement was progressive or retrograde, but in any case the American, in his political character, was a new variety of man.

The social movement was also decided. The war gave a severe shock to the Anglican sympathies of society, and peace seemed to widen the breach between European and American tastes. Interest in Europe languished after Napoleon's overthrow. France ceased to affect American opinion. England became an object of less alarm. Peace produced in the United States a social and economical revolution which greatly curtailed the influence of New England, and with it the social authority of Great Britain. The invention of the steamboat counterbalanced ocean commerce. The South and West gave to society a character more aggressively American than had been known before. That Europe, within certain limits, might tend toward American ideas was possible, but that America should under any circumstances follow the experiences of European development might thenceforward be reckoned as improbable. American character was formed, if not fixed.

The scientific interest of American history centred in national character, and in the workings of a society destined to become vast, in which individuals were important chiefly as types. Although this kind of interest was different from that of European history, it was at least as important to the world. Should history ever become a true science, it must expect to establish its laws, not from the complicated story of rival European nationalities, but from the economical evolution of a great democracy. North America was the most favorable field on the globe for the spread of a society so large, uniform, and isolated as to answer the purposes of science. There a single homogeneous society could easily attain proportions of three or four hundred million persons, under conditions of undisturbed growth.

In Europe or Asia, except perhaps in China, undisturbed social evolution had been unknown. Without disturbance, evolution seemed to cease. Wherever disturbance occurred, permanence was impossible. Every people in turn adapted itself to the law of necessity. Such a system as that of the United States could hardly have existed for half a century in Europe except under the protection of another power. In the fierce struggle characteristic of European society, systems were permanent in nothing except in the general law, that, whatever other character they might possess they must always be chiefly military.

The want of permanence was not the only or the most confusing obstacle to the treatment of European history as a science. The intensity of the struggle gave prominence to the individual, until the hero seemed all, society nothing; and what was worse for science, the men were far more interesting than the societies. In the dramatic view of history, the hero deserved more to be studied than the community to which he belonged; in truth, he was the society, which existed only to produce him and to perish with him. Against such a view historians were among the last to protest, and protested but faintly when they did so at all. They felt as strongly as their audiences that the highest achievements were alone worth remembering either in history or in art, and that a reiteration of commonplaces was commonplace. With all the advantages of European movement and color, few historians succeeded in enlivening or dignifying the lack of motive, intelligence, and morality, the helplessness characteristic of many long periods in the face of crushing problems, and the futility of human efforts to escape from difficulties religious, political, and social. In a period extending over four or five thousand years, more or less capable of historical treatment, historians were content to illustrate here and there the most dramatic moments of the most striking communities. The hero was their favorite. War was the chief field of heroic action, and even the history of England was chiefly the story of war.

The history of the United States promised to be free from such disturbances. War counted for little, the hero for less; on the people alone the eye could permanently rest. The steady growth of a vast population without the social distinctions that confused other histories,—without kings, nobles, or armies; without church, traditions, and prejudices,—seemed a subject for the man of science rather than for dramatists or poets. To scientific treatment only one great obstacle existed. Americans, like Europeans, were not disposed to make of their history a mechanical evolution. They felt that they even more than other nations needed the heroic element, because they breathed an atmosphere of peace and industry where heroism could seldom be displayed; and in unconscious protest against their own social conditions they adorned with imaginary qualities scores of supposed leaders, whose only merit was their faculty of reflecting a popular trait. Instinctively they clung to ancient history as though conscious that of all misfortunes that could befall the national character, the greatest would be the loss of the established ideals which alone ennobled human weakness. Without heroes, the national character of the United States had few charms of imagination even to Americans.

Historians and readers maintained Old-World standards. No historian cared to hasten the coming of an epoch when man should study his own history in the same spirit and by the same methods with which he studied the formation of a crystal. Yet history had its scientific as well as its human side, and in American history the scientific interest was greater than the human. Elsewhere the student could study under better conditions the evolution of the individual, but nowhere could he study so well the evolution of a race. The interest of such a subject exceeded that of any other branch of science, for it brought mankind within sight of its own end.

Travellers in Switzerland who stepped across the Rhine where it flowed from its glacier could follow its course among mediæval towns and feudal ruins, until it became a highway for modern industry, and at last arrived at a permanent equilibrium in the ocean. American history followed the same course. With prehistoric glaciers and mediæval feudalism the story had little to do; but from the moment it came within sight of the ocean it acquired interest almost painful. A child could find his way in a river-valley, and a hoy could float on the waters of

Holland; but science alone could sound the depths of the ocean, measure its currents, foretell its storms, or fix its relations to the system of Nature. In a democratic ocean science could see something ultimate. Man could go no further. The atom might move, but the general equilibrium could not change.

Whether the scientific or the heroic view were taken, in either case the starting-point was the same, and the chief object of interest was to define national character. Whether the figures of history were treated as heroes or as types, they must be taken to represent the people. American types were especially worth study if they were to represent the greatest democratic evolution the world could know. Readers might judge for themselves what share the individual possessed in creating or shaping the nation; but whether it was small or great, the nation could be understood only by studying the individual. For that reason, in the story of Jefferson and Madison individuals retained their old interest as types of character, if not as sources of power.

In the American character antipathy to war ranked first among political traits. The majority of Americans regarded war in a peculiar light, the consequence of comparative security. No European nation could have conducted a war, as the people of America conducted the War of 1812. The possibility of doing so without destruction explained the existence of the national trait, and assured its continuance. In politics, the divergence of America from Europe perpetuated itself in the popular instinct for peaceable methods. The Union took shape originally on the general lines that divided the civil from the military elements of the British constitution. The party of Jefferson and Gallatin was founded on dislike of every function of government necessary in a military system. Although Jefferson carried his pacific theories to an extreme, and brought about a military reaction, the reactionary movement was neither universal, violent, nor lasting; and society showed no sign of changing its convictions. With greater strength the country might acquire greater familiarity with warlike methods, but in the same degree was less likely to suffer any general change of habits. Nothing but prolonged intestine contests could convert the population of an entire continent into a race of warriors.

A people whose chief trait was antipathy to war, and to any system organized with military energy, could scarcely develop great results in national administration; yet the Americans prided themselves chiefly on their political capacity. Even the war did not undeceive them, although the incapacity brought into evidence by the war was undisputed, and was most remarkable among the communities which believed themselves to be most gifted with political sagacity. Virginia and Massachusetts by turns admitted failure in dealing with issues so simple that the newest societies, like Tennessee and Ohio, understood them by instinct. That incapacity in national politics should appear as a leading trait in American character was unexpected by Americans, but might naturally result from their conditions. The better test of American character was not political but social, and was to be found not in the government but in the people.

The sixteen years of Jefferson's and Madison's rule furnished international tests of popular intelligence upon which Americans could depend. The ocean was the only open field for competition among nations. Americans enjoyed there no natural or artificial advantages over Englishmen, Frenchmen, or Spaniards; indeed, all these countries possessed navies, resources, and experience greater than were to be found in the United States. Yet the Americans developed, in the course of twenty years, a surprising degree of skill in naval affairs. The evidence of their success was to be found nowhere so complete as in the avowals of Englishmen who knew best the history of naval progress. The American invention of the fast-sailing schooner or clipper was the more remarkable because, of all American inventions, this alone sprang from direct competition with Europe. During ten centuries of struggle the nations of Europe had labored to obtain superiority over each other in ship-construction, yet Americans instantly made improvements which gave them superiority, and which Europeans were unable immediately to imitate even after seeing them. Not only were American vessels better in model, faster in sailing, easier and quicker in handling, and more economical in working than the European, but they were also better equipped. The English complained as a grievance that the Americans adopted new and unwarranted devices in naval warfare; that their vessels were heavier and better constructed, and their missiles of unusual shape and improper use. The Americans resorted to expedients that had not been tried before, and excited a mixture of irritation and respect in the English service, until Yankee smartness became a national misdemeanor.

The English admitted themselves to be slow to change their habits, but the French were both quick and scientific; yet Americans did on the ocean what the French, under stronger inducements, failed to do. The French privateer preyed upon British commerce for twenty years without seriously injuring it; but no sooner did the American privateer sail from French ports, than the rates of insurance doubled in London, and an outcry for protection arose among English shippers which the Admiralty could not calm. The British newspapers were filled with assertions that the American cruiser was the superior of any vessel of its class, and threatened to overthrow England's supremacy on the ocean.

Another test of relative intelligence was furnished by the battles at sea. Instantly after the loss of the "Guerriere" the English discovered and complained that American gunnery was superior to their own. They explained their inferiority by the length of time that had elapsed since their navy had found on the ocean an enemy to fight. Every vestige of hostile fleets had been swept away, until, after the battle of Trafalgar, British frigates ceased practice with their guns. Doubtless the British navy had become somewhat careless in the absence of a dangerous enemy, but Englishmen were themselves aware that some other cause must have affected their losses. Nothing showed that Nelson's line-of-battle ships, frigates, or sloops were as a rule better fought than the "Macedonian" and "Java," the "Avon" and "Reindeer." Sir Howard Douglas, the chief authority on the subject, attempted in vain to explain British reverses by the deterioration of British gunnery. His analysis showed only that American gunnery was extraordinarily good. Of all vessels, the sloop-of-war,—on account of its smallness, its quick motion, and its more accurate armament of thirty-two-pound carronades,—offered the best test of relative gunnery, and Sir Howard Douglas in commenting upon the destruction of the "Peacock" and "Avon" could only say,—

"In these two actions it is clear that the fire of the British vessels was thrown too high, and that the ordnance of their opponents were expressly and carefully aimed at and took effect chiefly in the hull."

The battle of the "Hornet" and "Penguin" as well as those of the "Reindeer" and "Avon," showed that the excellence of American gunnery continued till the close of the war. Whether at point-blank range or at long-distance practice, the Americans used guns as they had never been used at sea before.

None of the reports of former British victories showed that the British fire had been more destructive at any previous time than in 1812, and no report of any commander since the British navy existed showed so much damage inflicted on an opponent in so short a time as was proved to have been inflicted on themselves by the reports of British commanders in the American war. The strongest proof of American superiority was given by the best British officers, like Broke, who strained every nerve to

maintain an equality with American gunnery. So instantaneous
and energetic was the effort that, according to the British historian of the war, "a British forty-six-gun frigate of 1813 was half
as effective again as a British forty-six-gun frigate of 1812;" and,
as he justly said, "the slaughtered crews and the shattered
hulks" of the captured British ships proved that no want of
their old fighting qualities accounted for their repeated and almost habitual mortifications.

Unwilling as the English were to admit the superior skill of
Americans on the ocean, they did not hesitate to admit it, in
certain respects, on land. The American rifle in American
hands was affirmed to have no equal in the world. This admission could scarcely be withheld after the lists of killed and
wounded which followed almost every battle; but the admission served to check a wider inquiry. In truth, the rifle played
but a small part in the war. Winchester's men at the river Raisin
may have owed their over-confidence, as the British Forty-first
owed its losses, to that weapon, and at New Orleans five or six
hundred of Coffee's men, who were out of range, were armed
with the rifle; but the surprising losses of the British were commonly due to artillery and musketry fire. At New Orleans the
artillery was chiefly engaged. The artillery battle of January 1,
according to British accounts, amply proved the superiority of
American gunnery on that occasion, which was probably the
fairest test during the war. The battle of January 8 was also
chiefly an artillery battle; the main British column never arrived within fair musket range; Pakenham was killed by a
grape-shot, and the main column of his troops halted more
than one hundred yards from the parapet.

The best test of British and American military qualities,
both for men and weapons, was Scott's battle of Chippawa.
Nothing intervened to throw a doubt over the fairness of the
trial. Two parallel lines of regular soldiers, practically equal in
numbers, armed with similar weapons, moved in close order

toward each other, across a wide open plain, without cover or advantage of position, stopping at intervals to load and fire, until one line broke and retired. At the same time two three-gun batteries, the British being the heavier, maintained a steady fire from positions opposite each other. According to the reports, the two infantry lines in the centre never came nearer than eighty yards. Major-General Riall reported that then, owing to severe losses, his troops broke and could not be rallied. Comparison of the official reports showed that the British lost in killed and wounded four hundred and sixty-nine men; the Americans, two hundred and ninety-six. Some doubts always affect the returns of wounded, because the severity of the wound cannot be known; but dead men tell their own tale. Riall reported one hundred and forty-eight killed; Scott reported sixty-one. The severity of the losses showed that the battle was sharply contested, and proved the personal bravery of both armies. Marksmanship decided the result, and the returns proved that the American fire was superior to that of the British in the proportion of more than fifty per cent if estimated by the entire loss, and of two hundred and forty-two to one hundred if estimated by the deaths alone.

The conclusion seemed incredible, but it was supported by the results of the naval battles. The Americans showed superiority amounting in some cases to twice the efficiency of their enemies in the use of weapons. The best French critic of the naval war, Jurien de la Gravière said: "An enormous superiority in the rapidity and precision of their fire can alone explain the difference in the losses sustained by the combatants." So far from denying this conclusion the British press constantly alleged it, and the British officers complained of it. The discovery caused great surprise, and in both British services much attention was at once directed to improvement in artillery and musketry. Nothing could exceed the frankness with which Englishmen avowed their inferiority. According to Sir Francis

Head, "gunnery was in naval warfare in the extraordinary state of ignorance we have just described, when our lean children, the American people, taught us, rod in hand, our first lesson in the art." The English text-book on Naval Gunnery, written by Major-General Sir Howard Douglas immediately after the peace, devoted more attention to the short American war than to all the battles of Napoleon, and began by admitting that Great Britain had "entered with too great confidence on war with a marine much more expert than that of any of our European enemies." The admission appeared "objectionable" even to the author; but he did not add, what was equally true, that it applied as well to the land as to the sea service.

No one questioned the bravery of the British forces, or the ease with which they often routed larger bodies of militia; but the losses they inflicted were rarely as great as those they suffered. Even at Bladensburg, where they met little resistance, their loss was several times greater than that of the Americans. At Plattsburg, where the intelligence and quickness of Macdonough and his men alone won the victory, his ships were in effect stationary batteries, and enjoyed the same superiority in gunnery. "The 'Saratoga,'" said his official report, "had fifty-five round-shot in her hull; the 'Confiance,' one hundred and five. The enemy's shot passed principally just over our heads, as there were not twenty whole hammocks in the nettings at the close of the action."

The greater skill of the Americans was not due to special training, for the British service was better trained in gunnery, as in everything else, than the motley armies and fleets that fought at New Orleans and on the Lakes. Critics constantly said that every American had learned from his childhood the use of the rifle, but he certainly had not learned to use cannon in shooting birds or hunting deer, and he knew less than the Englishman about the handling of artillery and muskets. As if to add unnecessary evidence, the battle of Chrystler's Farm proved only too well that this American efficiency was not confined to citizens of the United States.

Another significant result of the war was the sudden development of scientific engineering in the United States. This branch of the military service owed its efficiency and almost its existence to the military school at West Point, established in 1802. The school was at first much neglected by government. The number of graduates before the year 1812 was very small; but at the outbreak of the war the corps of engineers was already efficient. Its chief was Colonel Joseph Gardner Swift, of Massachusetts, the first graduate of the academy: Colonel Swift planned the defences of New York harbor. The lieutenant-colonel in 1812 was Walker Keith Armistead, of Virginia,—the third graduate, who planned the defences of Norfolk. Major William McRee, of North Carolina, became chief engineer to General Brown, and constructed the fortifications at Fort Erie, which cost the British General Gordon Drummond the loss of half his army, besides the mortification of defeat. Captain Eleazer Derby Wood, of New York, constructed Fort Meigs, which enabled Harrison to defeat the attack of Proctor in May, 1813. Captain Joseph Gilbert Totten, of New York, was chief engineer to General Izard at Plattsburg, where he directed the fortifications that stopped the advance of Prevost's great army. None of the works constructed by a graduate of West Point was captured by the enemy; and had an engineer been employed at Washington by Armstrong and Winder, the city would have been easily saved.

Perhaps without exaggeration the West Point Academy might be said to have decided, next to the navy, the result of the war. The works at New Orleans were simple in character, and as far as they were due to engineering skill were directed by Major Latour, a Frenchman; but the war was already ended when the battle of New Orleans was fought. During the critical campaign of 1814, the West Point engineers doubled the capacity of the little American army for resistance, and introduced a new and scientific character into American life.

In the application of science the steamboat was the most striking success; but Fulton's invention, however useful, was neither the most original nor the most ingenious of American efforts, nor did it offer the best example of popular characteristics. Perhaps Fulton's torpedo and Stevens's screw-propeller showed more originality than was proved by the "Clermont." The fast-sailing schooner with its pivot-gun—an invention that grew out of the common stock of nautical intelligence—best illustrated the character of the people.

That the individual should rise to a higher order either of intelligence or morality than had existed in former ages was not to be expected, for the United States offered less field for the development of individuality than had been offered by older and smaller societies. The chief function of the American Union was to raise the average standard of popular intelligence and well-being, and at the close of the War of 1812 the superior average intelligence of Americans was so far admitted that Yankee acuteness, or smartness, became a national reproach; but much doubt remained whether the intelligence belonged to a high order, or proved a high morality. From the earliest ages, shrewdness was associated with unscrupulousness; and Americans were freely charged with wanting honesty. The charge could neither be proved nor disproved. American morality was such as suited a people so endowed, and was high when compared with the morality of many older societies; but, like American intelligence, it discouraged excess. Probably the political morality shown by the government and by public men during the first sixteen years of the century offered a fair gauge of social morality. Like the character of the popular inventions, the character of the morals corresponded to the wants of a growing democratic society; but time alone could decide whether it would result in a high or a low national ideal.

Finer analysis showed other signs of divergence from ordinary standards. If Englishmen took pride in one trait more than in another, it was in the steady uniformity of their progress. The innovating and revolutionary quality of the French mind irritated them. America showed an un-English rapidity in movement. In politics, the American people between 1787 and 1817 accepted greater changes than had been known in England since 1688. In religion, the Unitarian movement of Boston and Harvard College would never have been possible in England, where the defection of Oxford or Cambridge, and the best educated society in the United Kingdom, would have shaken Church and State to their foundations. In literature the American school was chiefly remarkable for the rapidity with which it matured. The first book of Irving was a successful burlesque of his own ancestral history; the first poem of Bryant sang of the earth only as a universal tomb; the first preaching of Channing assumed to overthrow the Trinity; and the first paintings of Allston aspired to recover the ideal perfection of Raphael and Titian. In all these directions the American mind showed tendencies that surprised Englishmen more than they struck Americans. Allston defended himself from the criticism of friends who made complaint of his return to America. He found there, as he maintained, not only a growing taste for art, but "a quicker appreciation" of artistic effort than in any European land. If the highest intelligence of American society were to move with such rapidity, the time could not be far distant when it would pass into regions which England never liked to contemplate.

Another intellectual trait, as has been already noticed, was the disposition to relax severity. Between the theology of Jonathan Edwards and that of William Ellery Channing was an enormous gap, not only in doctrines but also in methods. Whatever might be thought of the conclusions reached by Edwards and Hopkins, the force of their reasoning commanded respect. Not often had a more strenuous effort than theirs been made to ascertain God's will, and to follow it without regard to weaknesses of the flesh. The idea that the nature of God's attributes was to be preached only as subordinate to the improvement of man, agreed little with the spirit of their religion. The Unitarian and Universalist movements marked the beginning of an epoch when ethical and humanitarian ideas took the place of metaphysics, and even New England turned from contemplating the omnipotence of the Deity in order to praise the perfections of his creatures.

The spread of great popular sects like the Universalists and Campbellites, founded on assumptions such as no Orthodox theology could tolerate, showed a growing tendency to relaxation of thought in that direction. The struggle for existence was already mitigated, and the first effect of the change was seen in the increasing cheerfulness of religion. Only when men found their actual world almost a heaven, could they lose overpowering anxiety about the world to come. Life had taken a softer aspect, and as a consequence God was no longer terrible. Even the wicked became less mischievous in an atmosphere where virtue was easier than vice. Punishments seemed mild in a society where every offender could cast off his past, and create a new career. For the first time in history, great bodies of men turned away from their old religion, giving no better reason than that it required them to believe in a cruel Deity, and rejected necessary conclusions of theology because they were inconsistent with human self-esteem.

The same optimism marked the political movement. Society was weary of strife, and settled gladly into a political system which left every disputed point undetermined. The public seemed obstinate only in believing that all was for the best, as far as the United States were concerned, in the affairs of mankind. The contrast was great between this temper of mind and that in which the Constitution had been framed; but it was no greater than the contrast in the religious opinions of the two periods, while the same reaction against severity marked the new literature. The rapid accumulation of wealth and increase in physical comfort told the same story from the standpoint of economy. On every side society showed that ease was for a time to take the place of severity, and enjoyment was to have its full share in the future national existence.

The traits of intelligence, rapidity, and mildness seemed fixed in the national character as early as 1817, and were likely to become more marked as time should pass. A vast amount of conservatism still lingered among the people; but the future spirit of society could hardly fail to be intelligent, rapid in movement, and mild in method. Only in the distant future could serious change occur, and even then no return to European characteristics seemed likely. The American continent was happier in its conditions and easier in its resources than the regions of Europe and Asia, where Nature revelled in diversity and conflict. If at any time American character should change, it might as probably become sluggish as revert to the violence and extravagances of Old-World development. The inertia of several hundred million people, all formed in a similar social mould, was as likely to stifle energy as to stimulate evolution.

With the establishment of these conclusions, a new episode in American history began in 1815. New subjects demanded new treatment, no longer dramatic but steadily tending to become scientific. The traits of American character were fixed; the rate of physical and economical growth was established; and history, certain that at a given distance of time the Union would contain so many millions of people, with wealth valued at so many millions of dollars, became thenceforward chiefly concerned to know what kind of people these millions were to be. They were intelligent, but what paths would their intelligence select? They were quick, but what solution of insoluble problems would quickness hurry? They were scientific, and what control would their science exercise over their destiny? They were mild, but what corruptions would their relaxations bring? They were peaceful, but by what machinery were their corruptions to be purged? What interests were to vivify a society so vast and uniform? What ideals were to ennoble it? What object, besides physical content, must a democratic continent aspire to attain? For the treatment of such questions, history required another century of experience.

TITLES IN SERIES